Applications for 3D Printing

KRISTIN THIEL

Cavendish
Square
New York

Library of Congress Cataloging-in-Publication Data

Names: Thiel, Kristin.
Title: Applications for 3D printing / Kristin Thiel.
Description: New York : Cavendish Square Publishing, 2018. | Series: Project learning with 3D printing | Includes bibliographical references and index.
Identifiers: ISBN 9781502631527 (library bound) | ISBN 9781502631534 (ebook)
Subjects: LCSH: Three-dimensional printing--Juvenile literature.
Classification: LCC TS171.95 T4527 2018 | DDC 621.9/88--dc23

Editorial Director: David McNamara
Editor: Fletcher Doyle
Copy Editor: Nathan Heidelberger
Associate Art Director: Amy Greenan
Designer: Alan Sliwinski
Production Coordinator: Karol Szymczuk
Photo Research: J8 Media

CONTENTS

1 Life-Altering Technology **5**

2 3D Printing at Home
   and in Space **25**

3 3D Printing in Everyday Life
   and on the Big Screen **49**

4 3D Printing in Health Care **71**

5 3D Printing in Forensics
   and Other Careers **93**

Glossary 114

Further Information 118

Index 124

About the Author 128

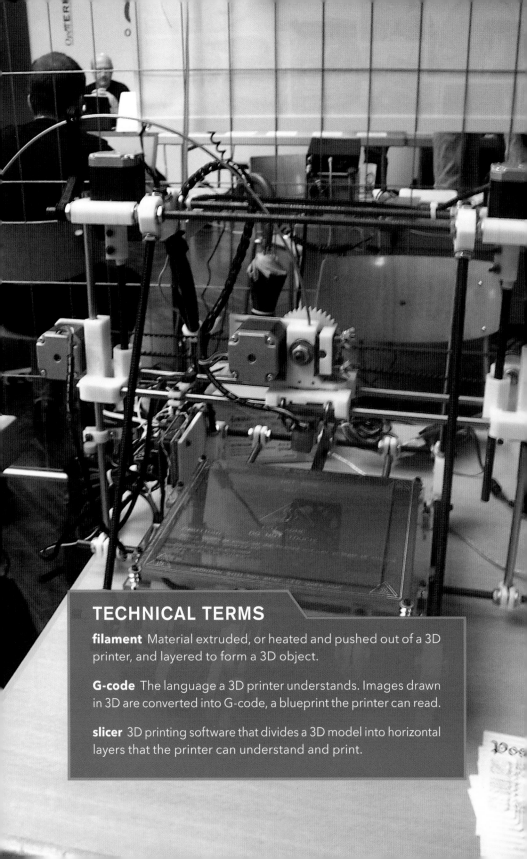

TECHNICAL TERMS

filament Material extruded, or heated and pushed out of a 3D printer, and layered to form a 3D object.

G-code The language a 3D printer understands. Images drawn in 3D are converted into G-code, a blueprint the printer can read.

slicer 3D printing software that divides a 3D model into horizontal layers that the printer can understand and print.

CHAPTER ONE

Life-Altering Technology

IN AN **ADDITIVE PROCESS**, AN OBJECT IS BUILT BY ADDING **layer** upon layer of material to create that object. **3D** printing is an additive process. Think of it like building a sand castle, layering sand upon sand until there's a building by the sea. Or, more accurately, 3D printing is like assembling a layer cake. You set one layer down on a platter, just like the 3D printer **extrudes** a liquified ribbon of material, such as plastic, onto the printer bed. Then you set another layer on top of the first; the printer **nozzle** returns to its starting point and lays down another layer of material on top of the first. In a moment, we'll briefly review that process and the history of the

Opposite: This 3D printer is ready for work at a conference for free software in France.

technology. But first, let's consider this book's specific focus, which is 3D printing's applications—how it's used, in what industries, by what people, and for what purposes.

Disruptive Technology

When we think about applying 3D printing to the world, using it to address our needs, we may consider 3D printing not only as an additive technology but as a "disruptive" one. That's the word that Abraham Reichental, former head of the 3D printer manufacturer 3D Systems, used to describe 3D printing. In his opinion, the technology will drastically alter, in the very best way, every part of life. According to his video interview with the *Financial Times* in 2012, 3D printing will be as important, and as world changing, as the steam engine, the computer, and the internet were in their early days. "It's going to change how we learn. It's going to change how we create. And it's going to change how we manufacture," he said.

The magazine *Kids, Code, and Computer Science* has offered some great examples of how pervasive, or always present, 3D printing could be in everyday life, focusing on the benefit to the environment. It's said that many of us live in a throwaway culture. Some products, like cell phones, are built to last only a couple of years. In other cases, even if an item could last a long time, if a part of it breaks, it can seem easier to just buy a new one than to fix it. Since we can shop in just a few clicks of the mouse, we're encouraged to buy instead of repair. But 3D printing is also possible with just a few keystrokes. If the plastic back of your TV remote cracks, *Kids, Code, and Computer Science* suggests that you could print a new back as easily as you could order a whole new remote, and for less money. Replacing the broken back definitely would mean less wear and tear on the environment, as you wouldn't throw the whole remote away.

Experts studying and making predictions about 3D printing agree that the technology is already a big deal and is only going to become bigger. According to a 2015 *Forbes* rundown of reports by industry leaders, the worldwide 3D printing arena was expected to grow by billions of dollars from year to year. The projections about that growth continue to be updated in dramatic ways. For example, the 2013 *Wohlers Report*, which reviewed and analyzed 3D printing, estimated that the field would grow to become a $10.8 billion industry by 2021. A year later, that report forecast a number nearly double the 2013 estimate, and for a shorter period of time: *Wohlers Report* 2014 said that worldwide revenue from 3D printing would exceed $21 billion by 2020. It also estimated that revenue would reach that number by taking great leaps over a short time frame. It calculated that the technology's annual revenue would jump an amazing four times from what it was in 2013, which was $3.07 billion, to $12.8 billion in only five years, by 2018. Financial expectations for 3D printing applications are hugely positive.

The reality of applying 3D printing to a variety of industries supports the projections. In his 2012 interview with the *Financial Times*, Reichental said that 3D printers weren't ready to print incredibly sturdy items, like jet engine parts. In 2016, General Electric started testing its new GE9X jet engine, made for the Boeing 777X, a commercial passenger plane. This engine was the largest, most efficient, and most powerful engine of its kind–and it also was made with 3D-printed parts. Within four years, exactly what Reichental hadn't expected to happen yet was actually happening.

In 2016, General Electric began 3D printing parts for the massive engine that propels the Boeing 777x.

A Basic Definition of 3D Printing

You can compare 3D printing to text printing, except instead of applying ink to paper in a pattern that forms letters that had been typed on a computer, 3D printers most commonly apply plastic in a pattern that forms the three-dimensional object drawn on a computer.

Objects are created in 3D printing by adding layers of material, not subtracting pieces from a bigger piece of material. The 3D printer lays down its material, its "ink," on a blank canvas that is the printer bed. By contrast, someone making a wooden bowl takes a block of wood and cuts and sands pieces away until a bowl shape is all that remains. There is a difference in cost between methods that add material and those that subtract material to make an object. (The latter is called **subtractive manufacturing**.) The cost of a 3D-printed bowl is the cost of the material that makes up that actual bowl. The cost of a carved wooden bowl is in reality the cost of the full block of wood, much of which was cut away and discarded.

Two-part **software** is required for 3D printing. The first part is the 3D printer front end. This software talks to your printer and helps it to process what you've designed on your computer and want to print. Popular open-source 3D printer front ends are Printrun/Pronterface, RepRap Host software, RepSnapper, and ReplicatorG. The second part of the software is a **slicer**, like Skeinforge, Slic3r, Cura, and KISSlicer. A slicer is

3D printing software that cuts the drawing of an object into horizontal layers. Picture that towering cake we thought of earlier, but covered in frosting. If you scrape the frosting off, you see that the baker had to prepare multiple individual layers to create such a tall cake.

A slicer approaches your 3D model as though it were constructing a layer cake, breaking the image into layers to print one at a time. Each corresponding layer is then converted into **G-code**. G-code is the language through which you tell your 3D printer what to do for every layer of the print.

3D PRINTING TIP

A level **build bed** (also called a printer bed) is crucial for a good print. You will need to level the bed of a new printer, and you'll have to level it as part of regular maintenance. According to Pinshape, three errors may indicate an unleveled bed: the first layer of **filament** isn't sticking to the bed well; your layers are inconsistent in thickness; or plastic gathers around the nozzle.

The 3D Printing Process

Printing a three-dimensional object is an idea similar to printing a page of text, but it is a much more complicated process. These are the basic steps:

- Find a model or draw your own with **computer-aided design (CAD)** software.

- Review your design. This is as important a step as the drawing of the object because it means the difference between your idea staying an image and becoming an object. If you write a terrible short story, one that no one would ever want to read, or even one that was complete gibberish, you could still print it. Ink in the form of letters and words would be present on a piece of paper, and you could hand that paper to someone and they'd believe, at least before they read it, that they'd been given a story. 3D printing is different. If you draw something that looks like a toy car but you make the outline too thin, the roof may collapse. If you forget to draw the car's underside, the printer won't see it as a complete object and can't print it. Remembering to draw your object as a solid is called making your object **watertight**. Imagine filling the toy car with water—would it leak? If it would, what your 3D printer produces won't look like a toy car.
- Save your model as an **STL** file, then open it in a slicer that converts your model into a G-code the 3D printer understands.
- Print. To do so, the 3D printer must do a lot of work. It takes material, often plastic rope coiled around a spool, and heats the material so that it can extrude, or push, it out onto the printer bed, methodically layering the material into a three-dimensional object. Before and during this stage,

3D PRINTING PIONEERS

Despite the fact that 3D printing feels like a very modern invention, it has roots in the 1980s. In 1988, the printing of a plastic-and-wax frog to amuse a two-year-old child was one of the technology's first practical applications.

S. Scott Crump was the designer of that frog. At the time, he was an aviation engineer in his mid-thirties who was frustrated with how long it took and how much it cost to make a **prototype**. He wondered if the 2D plotter, a type of computer printer that he used to create 3D images, could be redesigned to go one step further and create 3D objects.

According to the Minnesota Inventors Hall of Fame website, Crump turned his home kitchen into a lab to test his idea. He loaded a hot glue gun with **polyethylene** and candle wax and then squeezed the warm goo, layer by layer, into the shape of a frog (which he later presented to his daughter). He automated the process by redesigning a 2D plotter to print wax and plastic instead of its usual ink. He practiced so much that food cooked in the kitchen started tasting vaguely of plastic, so he moved his experiments to the garage.

After he had spent $10,000 on equipment, his wife, Lisa, suggested they turn his hobby into a business. They cofounded 3D printer manufacturer Stratasys Inc. in 1989.

He soon had invented a machine that could make a prototype within hours, but the whole kit cost $130,000, and no company was interested in taking such an expensive leap into 3D printing. Stratasys's first salable printer was shipped in 1991; the next year, the company sold four printers. Now, it owns MakerBot and GrabCAD, two leaders in 3D printing. As of 2012, Stratasys's revenues were $350 million; the next year, according to Crump in *Silicon Hills News*, the company made $487 million. In 2014, it pioneered the color 3D printer as well as one that could print in multiple materials. The company's products are used in the fields of aerospace, defense, automotive, medical, business and industrial equipment, education, architecture, and consumer products.

Scott Crump has a mechanical engineering degree from Washington State University and a master's degree in entrepreneurial studies from the University of California, Los Angeles (UCLA). Lisa Crump has a bachelor's degree from Washington State University and master's degree from Portland State University. She has completed business trainings and certifications at UCLA's Anderson School of Management and Wharton Business School.

Scott Crump was the only person to be inducted into the Minnesota Inventors Hall of Fame in 2014. Established in 1976, this group identifies Minnesotans who have made significant contributions through their inventions. In addition to heading up many aspects of their business, Lisa Crump supports related community-based nonprofits, focusing on those that encourage kids in STEM classes and fields and those that support women in building businesses.

you need to do a lot of work. Precision is critical, so you may need to adjust your printer. A printer of text can produce something readable even if a part is slightly askew. A person can read an angled line of text or one that is slightly smudged. On a 3D printer, the print head, pulleys, and extruder hardware must be aligned, and software dimensions must be translated to the correct real-world dimensions used by the printer hardware. If your printed object doesn't look right, you may need to adjust the hardware–the 3D printer–or the design.

Materials Used in 3D Printing

According to 3D Printing Industry, while plastics remain common materials for 3D printers, many different types of materials (even metal and glass) in many different forms (not just glue-like ribbons but powder and pellets) can be "printed" in layers–and applications are driving the development of many of those. If an industry would like to 3D print an item to make work more efficient or its products more successful, researchers are finding ways to print in that industry's main material.

A Pioneering Application

Manufacturing was an early adopter of 3D printing. Prototyping–testing out an idea in its actual product form—becomes rapid prototyping with 3D printing. The technology allows manufacturers to create real objects directly from CAD designs, which means feedback on designs and subsequent revisions of them can come quicker than ever. This helps ideas become successful products more quickly. Stratasys explains on its website why 3D printing is so useful for rapid prototyping.

3D PRINTING TIP

Just like thread can get tangled as it is unwound from its spool, filament can become tangled or experience other problems moving freely from its spool during a 3D print. Making improvements to the spool or where you've placed it before printing is a good idea. Some filament manufacturers may offer higher-quality spools than others.

Because no design is perfect the first time it is translated into a product, testing, feedback, and revision are necessary. Stratasys says that 3D printing offers the "flexibility required to make this crucial trial and error process possible for physical products." And because the earlier a problem is found, the easier it is to fix it, 3D printing is great because it "allows industrial designers and engineers more revisions in less time, so they can test thoroughly while still reducing time to market."

A drawing or a photograph can only convey so much to clients. If someone can hold a three-dimensional object in his or her hands, it is easier to see issues and ask for revisions. Related to this, manufacturers can study how the actual product will do in the real world. How does the design stand up to exterior forces? What if the design were printed in metal instead of **thermoplastic**? Providing answers to these questions in order to "prove out your products and manufacturing processes before making big investments" is what 3D printing does best for the manufacturing industry.

Manufacturers continue to agree that 3D printing is useful. According to a 2015 *Forbes* rundown of reports by industry leaders, the majority–67 percent–of manufacturers were using 3D printing. Of those surveyed in a recent Gartner study, 37 percent had one 3D printer within their organizations; 18 percent owned ten or more. The average number of printers per organization was 5.4. Nearly a quarter of organizations, 24.6 percent, were using 3D printing for prototyping.

Behind-the-Scenes Numbers

Math and 3D printing go hand in hand. Mathematical formulas work behind the scenes to create software programs, and geometry is needed to design objects. In return, 3D printing can help people understand complex math. Thanks to 3D printing, even the biggest of mathematical concepts can be seen, held, and even physically manipulated–quite literally. The math behind shapes can be seen in 3D-printed objects. You can apply that knowledge to hobbies and jobs such as photography.

In his 2016 book, *Visualizing Mathematics with 3D Printing*, Henry Segerman used 3D-printed objects to explain complex geometric concepts like symmetry, circular paraboloids, and four-dimensional shapes. Segerman, a mathematician, calculated the formulas for different shapes and then translated them into G-code for a 3D printer. This gave him physical models of everything from gnarled knots to hyperbolic honeycombs, a great way to visualize and touch what complicated math tries to express. His book helps "to explain mathematical concepts that are incomprehensible without an advanced degree," says *Wired*. For example, with Segerman's examples, someone could "do four dimensional math without actually being able to perceive the fourth dimension." It's pretty cool that 3D printing can help you actually do math beyond your understanding.

Mathematicians have always relied on models to help them understand their theories, but in the past, they've had to do things like carve wood or make plaster molds of the shapes. One math professor told *Wired* that she used to haunt her local hardware store for scraps with which to fashion peculiar shapes. 3D printing allows her to make shapes faster and to share them more widely, as Segerman has done. Readers of his book can find 3D images of the shapes online, buy 3D printed versions, or download steps to 3D print their own. Segerman's approach also helps people with aphantasia, the inability to visualize mental images. People with aphantasia can't call to mind what a sphere, like a ball or globe, looks like without one in front of them. Segerman himself has aphantasia.

While *Visualizing Mathematics with 3D Printing* helps readers see the mathematics behind objects by moving from formula to physical object, it also moves in the other direction, by showing the simple shapes at the foundation of the complicated ones. Using stereographic projection, shining a light source, like a flashlight, down at a sphere, Segerman projected the sphere's shadow

Professor Henry Segerman demonstrates his work during an exhibition on 3D-printed geometric objects and their two-dimensional shadows.

onto the table below. This projection mapped the 2D surface of a 3D ball onto a 2D plane.

Not only does this help students of math understand even complicated forms as simple structures folded, turned, twisted, or curved, but it also is useful in understanding certain activities and jobs outside of the math department. Some camera fisheye lenses use a stereographic projection to capture a wide angle. This is cool because stereographic projection is conformal–it preserves angles. A photo taken with this kind of lens is curved, so distances are distorted, but the details of buildings, for example, are exactly what they'd be with a high-zoom lens. Being able to understand how spheres flatten into 2D planes, and vice versa, is also important in cartography, which is mapmaking. Angle-preserving maps, the image created if you could shine a flashlight down upon the Earth and onto a piece of paper, are very useful for navigation purposes. Segerman himself is using his 3D experiments to make math games that feel nothing like school. His quintessence puzzles, as he's named them, let people play with "shadows" of four-dimensional objects. He's also working with research group EleVR on virtual reality experiences like his 4D Pac-Man-like game called Hypernom.

3D Printing Nature

The following chapters detail lots of practical applications for 3D printing, but let's end this chapter with applications that are both very grounded–in science and better understanding the natural world around us– as well as rather creative and artistic in look and feel.

Pollinators' Choice

Pollinators, like birds and bees, help plants make fruit or seeds. They move pollen from one part of a plant to another, which fertilizes the plant. Scientists know that the work of these pollinators has helped to evolve traits in plants. For example, if a bird species has a thick beak on which it might transfer the pollen, the species of flower it is attracted to might slowly, over time, evolve to have a bloom that is wide enough to accept the beak. Scientists also know that pollinators themselves must adapt to the flowers they crave. But it's been difficult to study flowers and animals alike–why and how they do what they do–until a development in 3D printing in 2015.

According to an article out of the University of Washington (UW), ecologists have been limited to breeding plants already known about in nature or handcrafting papier-mâché flower shapes in order to study how pollinators interact with them. The latter isn't an efficient way to build flowers, nor does it allow for standardization. By the very nature of being handmade, one flower will be at least slightly different from another, and one scientist could not accurately replicate another scientist's work.

Then UW biology graduate student Eric Octavio Campos led a team of students to 3D print flowers, and the possibilities opened. They made one set of flowers to look like trumpets and another to look like CDs or records, flat with a hole in the middle. They filled the flowers with "nectar," sugar water, and released hawk moths in the room to see which flower shape the moths preferred.

The hawk moth was a fascinating creature for the students to study. It poses a common concern in the United States because its larvae eat tobacco plants in the South. It also is large, the size of a human fist, with a long beak, and it is nocturnal, doing its work at night.

Campos explained to UWToday why he wanted to know how these animals manage to pollinate anything. "Imagine being given a garden hose that's almost twice your height in length. Now imagine trying to thread the other end through a hole that's scarcely wider than the hose itself—at dusk as the sun is setting or at night during a full moon." The work the hawk moths do to pollinate is amazing.

Because the moths fed from the trumpet-shaped 3D-printed flowers, the researchers concluded that the moths use touch rather than sight to find nectar.

Flight of a Moth, Dance of a Silkworm

3D printing helps us understand the natural world, and the natural world helps us improve 3D printing technology. For his master of fine arts program at London's Royal College of Art, Geoffrey Mann trapped a moth inside a light fixture and then 3D printed its path.

Flowers can be precisely replicated for study with a 3D printer.

He crafted the frenetic but beautiful plastic swoops into an avant-garde lamp. We have to wonder what being able to see such a complex flight path might tell biologists and others who study the natural world. Clues to animal behavior and how to better support the environment around us might lie in part with being able to print out complicated geometry like that.

According to a 2013 *Dezeen* article, architect Neri Oxman and her team of Massachusetts Institute of Technology (MIT) researchers at the Mediated Matter group, which focuses on nature-inspired design and design-inspired nature, have come to see silkworms as useful models for multiaxial 3D printers that use multiple materials at once. Silkworms "print" their cocoons by moving their heads in figure eights, extruding silk fibers and sericin, a gumlike substance that seals the fibers together. That alone is cool, but what really ups the game is they're able to control the ratio of the material and to vary the gradient of the printed material, so the cocoon has a soft interior and a hard exterior.

Oxman and her team "attached tiny magnets to a silkworm's head," she told *Dezeen*, "and we motion-tracked its movement as it built its cocoon. We then translated the data to a 3D printer connected to a robotic arm, which would allow us to examine the biological structure in a larger scale."

Next, we look at 3D printing being applied to home and travel—both on Earth and in outer space.

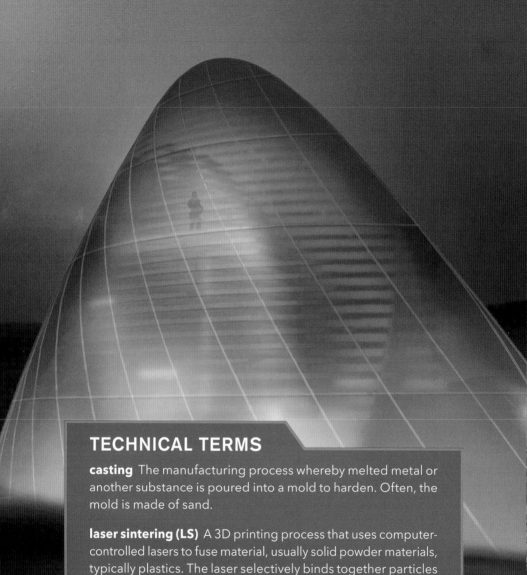

TECHNICAL TERMS

casting The manufacturing process whereby melted metal or another substance is poured into a mold to harden. Often, the mold is made of sand.

laser sintering (LS) A 3D printing process that uses computer-controlled lasers to fuse material, usually solid powder materials, typically plastics. The laser selectively binds together particles by raising the powder temperature.

3D sand printing This method makes casts in which to pour liquid metal to make a metal object. A resin binder "glues" layers of silica sand, cerabeads, or zirconia together to make the mold.

CHAPTER TWO

3D Printing at Home and in Space

I N THIS CHAPTER, WE EXPLORE 3D PRINTING APPLICATIONS FROM close to home to the farthest borders of human travel. Architects, who design homes, office buildings, and other living and working structures, were some of the earliest users of 3D printing, and they continue to expand the boundaries of what's possible with the technology. The airline and automotive industries are innovators with 3D printing, making their products lighter, stronger, and more cost effective. The technology is even going into space, allowing astronauts to make their own replacement tools and other needed items without returning to Earth.

Opposite: The 3D-printed Mars Ice House won first prize in a space-habitat competition in 2015.

Architecture: Early Adopter

Business News Daily wrote back in 2013 that "3D printing will disrupt businesses, particularly those that rely heavily on blueprinting or prototyping." Lira Luis, chief collaboration architect at Atelier Lira Luis LLC, a Chicago-based architecture and design firm, explained to *Business News Daily* that paper documents will disappear as 3D printers continue "quickly, inexpensively, and accurately printing a blueprint, in other words, a model, which can then be revised or followed to print final products."

Architecture was one of the earliest adopters of 3D printing technology. In fact, SketchUp, a 3D modeling software and one of the most popular entry points to 3D design, was developed for architects. Remnants from its past remain, as SketchUp can experience glitches when designs incorporate details smaller than one-sixteenth of an inch (1.6 millimeters). (Architects rarely need geometry smaller than one-sixteenth of an inch, so SketchUp was set up to read only larger designs.)

Piet Meijs, a senior associate at Rietveld Architects in New York City, explained in a Stratasys video that 3D printing is a "game changer" for architecture for several reasons: it increases efficiency; it allows for more variety in design; and it adds a "wow" factor to projects. Architecture is a competitive business. For every one construction job, there are several architecture firms bidding to be the designers. "Having a 3D printer separates you from the rest," Meijs explained. His firm credits its 3D printer with earning them jobs.

The first reason 3D printing is useful, Meijs said, is that it improves efficiency in the design stage. Architects draw building plans and then make 3D models of them so clients can get a truer sense of the proposed structure. Before 3D printing technology, architects constructed models by hand, which took a long time and was labor intensive. Because model building took so many resources, it was done toward the end of the design stage of the project. There was no time to spend on modeling a concept that may not be close to the final design. They also made only one model. They could not afford to allocate resources to handcraft multiple 3D models. With 3D printing, cost of materials to make a model is lower, as is the amount of time needed to make one. As for human labor, all that's required to construct a 3D model, after the design is drawn, is a push of the button to send the drawing to the printer. Because of this, architects can make models throughout the design process, allowing clients to review and discuss revisions from the very beginning. They also can make multiple copies of the model, so clients don't have to share one within their office and so they can distribute them to other key people. For example, the client may be the company that's going to be housed in the new office building, but it'd be nice if the mayor of the city where that building is going to be built could see the proposed structure early in the process.

Being able to experiment with scale is another reason to 3D print, Meijs said. The most successful construction projects have been examined in relation to nearby buildings and even the overall city. Architects can print models of different sizes and set them within printed models of their city block, so review boards can approve or revise the overall look.

3D PRINTING TIP

Coming up with an idea of what to print can be difficult. Consider thinking about what you could make that would make life better for another person. *IFLScience* reported on WASP, an Italian 3D printing company that is experimenting not only with printing shelters for the houseless but with doing so using material readily available where those people are, such as mud.

The "wow" factor, a third reason to print, is not to be discounted. Meijs talked about a project that completely changed direction midway through the process, so the client asked his firm to revise its plans. When Rietveld Architects came back two weeks later with not only drawings but also new 3D-printed models, the client knew they could trust the firm to meet any challenge with a quality response.

The client, not the architect, is the driver of the industry, Meijs said. Before computers, architects drew building plans by hand, but for years now, no client has accepted hand-drawn plans—a computer-aided design is the expected standard. Meijs believes the same will be true of 3D printing in architecture. Soon enough, no client will accept drawings only—they will want to see 3D models from the first step in a project through to breaking ground.

Architect Neri Oxman, who works out of MIT, has suggested that 3D printing is ushering in a third distinct era of construction technology. The first era was handcrafted production. "The craftsman," she told *Dezeen's Print Shift* publication on 3D printing, "had an almost phenomenological knowledge of materials and intuited how to vary their properties according to their structural and environmental characteristics." With the Industrial Revolution came a shift to the second era, in which machines and standardization took over. Industrial standards guided what and how we designed. Oxman has been excited about the emergence of a third era, one driven by 3D printing, where "craft meets the machine in rapid fabrication."

One need look no further than to architect Zaha Hadid to believe that 3D printing is good for both form and function in architecture. She was "renowned for her disregard for dull functionality and penchant for experimentation," according to the newspaper the *Independent*. Her "futuristic" buildings were "structurally intricate." In 2004, the Iraqi-born British architect became the first woman to win the Pritzker Architecture Prize, and following her death in 2016, she was honored with a Google Doodle in 2017. That same year, her architecture firm revealed its latest work

Zaha Hadid Architects created this experimental structure, titled *Thallus*, through 3D printing.

using 3D printing. *Thallus*, named for a Greek word for a type of plant, is a sculpture of strips of polylactide plastic. According to *Arch Daily*, a six-axis robotic 3D printer extruded the 4.3-mile- (7-kilometer-) long strip that looped around to connect with itself. The result was the "continuous, calla lily–like geometry" that is created through one single stroke. The work seems to honor Hadid's memory perfectly, as it "demonstrates what can now be achieved in terms of mechanization and customization in the architecture, construction and engineering industries."

Houses and 3D Printing

In January 2013, Universe Architecture, in the Netherlands, shared its plans to 3D print a two-story house out of concrete. The firm enlisted the help of Italian robotics engineer Enrico Dini, inventor of a 3D printer that uses sand and a chemical binding agent to create a stonelike material and that can print very large objects in one piece. Dini brought not only his printer but his know-how to Universe Architecture's project. In 2009, he printed, in sections that he later assembled, the first architectural structure. That was a nearly

The Big Delta 12m printer, one of the world's largest, is designed to print houses.

10-foot- (3-meter-) high egg-shaped pavilion designed by architect Andrea Morgante. A year later, along with designer Marco Ferreri, Dini was the first to print a house in one piece. It was a one-room hut with a door and two square windows.

Dini's 3D printer, called D-Shape, was once the largest 3D printer in the world. It works like this: First, a moving horizontal gantry, or framework, deposits a 5-millimeter (0.2-inch) layer of sand mixed with magnesium oxide, a white solid. Second, a row of nozzles squirts chlorine onto the areas of sand that are to become solid. Chlorine plus magnesium oxide creates a chemical reaction that turns sand into man-made sandstone. The two-step process repeats until the layers have built up into a three-dimensional structure.

3D PRINTING TIP

When you're considering what 3D printing process to use, think not only about budget and what type of material would be best for your object, but also about what type of material would be best for your environment. If you are 3D printing outside because you're building something larger, you may not want to layer powder because the wind could easily blow the granules away before you fuse, or "glue," them together.

Printing at a rate of 5 centimeters (2 inches) per hour, D-Shape can cover 30 square meters (323 square feet) to a depth of up to 2 meters (6.5 feet). This means that it can, at its most efficient, produce 30 cubic meters (1,059 cubic feet) of building per week.

For Universe Architecture's Landscape House, the firm has collaborated with the Royal BAM Group to create a robotic printer modeled after Dini's D-Shape printer. As of June 2017 the collaboration had not built the house, but it had completed a city bench in Amsterdam in the same shape. The shape is a continuous loop, with no beginning and no end.

This printer replaced a model that would print a form into which concrete is poured. Some firms don't think that's true 3D printing. One such critic, the now defunct Softkill Design, made **laser-sintering (LS)** machines to create parts of structures that didn't need concrete filler. Laser-sintered bioplastic, as thin as 0.7 millimeters (0.03 inches), was printed in a pattern akin to that of how bones grow. "We created an algorithm that mimics bone growth, so that we're depositing material only where it's necessary and most structurally efficient," Softkill Design's Aaron Silver told *Dezeen*'s *Print Shift* in 2013.

The firm planned to print a house in pieces and then transport the pieces to the site where the building was to stand. The fibrous strands of the pieces would hook together like Velcro when the pieces are pushed together.

The future of 3D-printed buildings is probably a mix of printing and weaving techniques, some experts believe. Neri Oxman told *Dezeen*'s *Print Shift* that, to her, 3D printing is defined primarily as "an approach for organizing material." To Oxman, the definition is open enough that there's impressive room for progress. Architectural technology will advance when we consider all kinds of materials, including responsive materials that adapt with the environment; all kinds of tools, from a solo-operating gantry to a "swarm" of robot printers; and all kinds of techniques, like 3D layering through weaving.

Cars and 3D Printing

Because LS production makes strong, water- and air-tight, and heat-resistant parts, this is a great technology for the automotive industry. Comedian and late-night talk-show host Jay Leno, now sharing his love of cars on his television show *Jay Leno's Garage*, spoke with Bry Ewan, a metals product manager for Stratasys Direct Manufacturing (SDM), about how to print metal parts for his large collection of classic cars.

Once a drawing of the part is made using CAD software, a 400-watt fiber laser microwelds metal powder into a solid metal object, from a heat- and corrosion-resistant nickel-chromium superalloy to titanium-64 and aluminum. According to 3DPrint.com, "The technology can create complex geometries that you can't get from other metal manufacturing processes, and it also gets rid of time-consuming tooling. The parts are strong and durable, and are also denser than investment casted metal parts. The process offers accuracy and

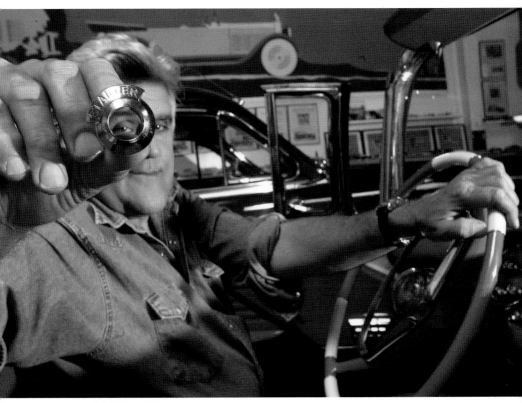

Jay Leno displays a part for a classic car that was 3D printed in metal by Stratasys.

fine feature detail." The cost was $500 to $600 per vertical inch.

Ford was an early adopter of 3D printing. In 1986, the car manufacturer bought the third 3D printer made. Now, the company has an entire lab devoted to the technology. In the lab are 3D-printed car parts as well as 3D-printed tools invented to help build these new parts. Not only do its engineers and technicians experiment with LS but they also are expanding their knowledge of ways to use **fused deposition modeling (FDM)** and **3D sand printing**. The processes create new parts layer by layer, "stacking up cross sections like a deck of playing cards," Ford's website explains.

Since that first 3D printer, Ford has printed more than five hundred thousand parts and saved billions of dollars and millions of hours. For example, a prototype that once took a quarter to half a year to build at a cost of half a million dollars now takes hours or days and only a few thousand dollars. This translates to car customers because prototypes are used to test every single part of the vehicle. If the testing costs less, the final product will also cost less.

Planes and 3D Printing

According to a 2017 article in *Ozy*, "Commercial aviation is ripe for disruption," and "the possibilities of 3D printing have emboldened ... engineers to create all-new engine designs that are ripping up the rulebook." Aviation is at a turning point because it's about to become more popular than ever among more people than ever. The International Air Transport Association has predicted that the number of air travelers will be 7.2 billion by 2035, and Boeing saw that as equaling the need for more than thirty-eight thousand new aircraft over the next twenty years. 3D printing may provide the answer to this burst because it can produce high-performing airplane components at much lower costs than traditional methods. "While many companies are jumping onboard the 3D printing train," 3DPrinting.com writes, "nowhere is there more buzz than in aviation."

In 2015, researchers at Northwestern University's McCormick School of Engineering who had been studying 3D printing's effect on aircraft efficiency explained that 3D-printed aircraft parts are much lighter and higher performing than traditional parts. This reduces the weight of airplanes, which in turn decreases carbon emissions and fuel consumption. Money is also saved using 3D printing at the production level. Conventional manufacturing wastes a lot of raw materials; by definition, 3D printing needs only what it uses—there is no waste. Eric Masanet, the lead Northwestern researcher, told 3DPrinting.com that even if manufacturers could 3D print only airplane brackets, hinges, seat buckles, and furniture, they could reduce the weight of an aircraft by 7 percent. This would be enough to save a noticeable amount on fuel, as much as 6.4 percent. This would be good for the financial bottom line as well as our environmental goals. Greenhouse gas emissions would decrease, and manufactures could save "thousands of tons of aluminum, titanium, and nickel that are otherwise scrapped every year."

As much as the aviation industry needs fiscally and environmentally friendly solutions, it also needs innovation support. If it can innovate, create, and advance more quickly and efficiently, lower costs and greener components will follow. And 3D printing is an inventor's dream technology. 3DPrinting.com quotes a General Electric (GE) report as saying, "It would normally take GE several years to design and prototype this part, but the GE team was able to shave as much as a year from the process." Bill Millhelm, a program manager for GE Aviation, said in the report, "The 3D printer allowed us to rapidly prototype the part, find the best design, and move it quickly to production ... We could never do this using the traditional **casting** process." Jonathan Clarke, another program manager, said that the 3D printed design was "faster and simpler" and with "superior material properties." He said, "This technology is a breakthrough."

3D-Printed Jet Parts

Aviation engineers aren't focusing on brackets and seats only. In April 2017, Boeing announced a venture with Norsk Titanium to print four titanium alloy parts for the frame of its 787 aircraft. These are the first printed structural components approved for use by the Federal Aviation Administration (FAA). Two years before, in 2015, the FAA cleared for flight GE's first 3D-printed part, a fist-sized T25 housing for a compressor inlet temperature sensor. Boeing and Norsk were to ask for approval to print more parts in 2018. With the technology cutting Boeing's costs by as much as $3 million per plane, 3DPrinting.com says it "would be a major boon for the industry."

Also in 2015, GE started testing a jet engine, the GE9X, for the efficient twin-engine Boeing 777X. It wasn't strange that it was the largest such engine ever built and that it was highly efficient and powerful compared with others. After all, GE was the first American company to build a jet engine, in 1942. What was unusual about this endeavor was that the engine was constructed with 3D-printed components.

According to an article in *Quartz*, the engine was 11 feet (3.35 meters) in diameter and generated 100,000 pounds (45 metric tons) of thrust. To those who say 3D printing can't produce strong products, this engine offered proof otherwise: it put out thrust equal to about one-third the force of the space shuttle's main engine. Alone, the nineteen 3D-printed fuel nozzles, which spray fuel inside the combustion chamber, helped reduce weight by 25 percent. This increased fuel efficiency, quieted the engine, and made the engine hugely popular. Five years before the engine's scheduled 2020 production date, GE had already received seven hundred orders, worth $29 billion.

Two years later, in May 2017, China's first 168-seat commercial plane with a 3D-printed engine successfully completed a test flight. According to an article in 3DPrint.com, this feat was a part of the Made in China 2025 plan, which aims to grow the country's manufacturing. Of the ten business sectors the plan focuses on, 3D printing is key. "The jet's maiden flight is showcasing 3D printing technology as a major role model in the country's manufacturing sector," according to 3DPrint.com. China hopes to increase the local manufacturing of parts to 90 percent; this "aggressive development" of the country's aviation industry will by necessity develop the 3D printing industry. China's metal 3D printer market was 181 units in 2016, and the country intends to grow that by four times in three years.

3D Printing in Space

At 1:52 a.m. on September 23, 2014, NASA sent a 3D printer into space. Appropriately for such a technology, which is all science but sometimes can seem magical, the printer rode in the Dragon Capsule of the SpaceX CRS-4. The printer that arrived in the belly of a dragon at the International Space Station (ISS), an internationally owned science lab about 220 miles (354 kilometers) above Earth, was developed by Made in Space, Inc., under a contract with NASA's Marshall Space Flight Center (MSFC).

Founded in 2010, Made In Space seeks "to develop solutions to commercial, industrial, research and defense challenges" by focusing on how objects are used in, and react to, space. Specifically, they focus on **additive manufacturing** technology for use in zero gravity. Entrepreneurs, space experts, and 3D printing developers spent more than thirty thousand hours testing 3D printers and completed more than four hundred parabolas of microgravity test flights before receiving clearance from NASA for launch. According to Aaron Kemmer, chief executive officer of Made in Space, in an article with 3D *Printer World*, "dozens of specific problems" had to be solved before a 3D printer could be ready for space. One of those was determining which type of 3D printing to use. They settled on a fused deposition modeling process, Quincy Bean, the principal investigator for the 3D Printing in Zero-G Project, told *Motherboard*, because "the filament is very easy to control in zero gravity." Without gravity, other 3D printing processes, such as those that use powder or resin, would cause serious issues in space. A powder bed would become "a powder cloud," and the vat of resin "would just be a big ball floating around."

The printer was sent to space specifically to demonstrate that on-site, on-demand manufacturing will be possible in space, and that will help the space program advance its programs. "Everything that has ever been built for space has been built on the ground," Kemmer told 3D *Printer World*. "This new capability will fundamentally change how the supply and development of space missions is looked at."

In 2014 and 2015, NASA conducted an experiment to understand the differences in 3D printing on Earth and in space. Scientists printed twenty-one items in conventional gravity conditions and the same objects far above Earth's atmosphere, on that 3D printer on the

NASA sent Made in Space's 3D printer into space in 2014, and it performed normally.

ISS. After the space-printed objects returned to Earth in early 2015, scientists put all the objects through a series of tests, comparing strength and durability, among other factors. According to 3D *Printer World*, 3D printing "is considered a potentially crucial component of extended space exploration." If astronauts could print their own replacement parts and tools, they could travel farther from Earth.

An early printing job that particularly delighted scientists both on the ground and in space was NASA's twentieth 3D printing experiment and the first time scientists on Earth emailed plans to space for a spur-of-the-moment need. Mike Chen, the cofounder of Made in Space, said he'd been listening to communication between the ISS and NASA when he heard ISS Commander Barry Wilmore mention that he needed a unique wrench for his work. "So we designed one in CAD and sent it up to him faster than a rocket ever could have." Because the printer was operated from a mission control ground station in California, all they did was type some commands on their computer, which sent a design of a ratcheting socket wrench in G-code to the ISS printer.

After hardware was tested on parabolic flights from Earth, items including those designed by students were printed on the ISS. This proved that a 3D printer can work normally in space.

3D Printing in Ice in Space

Also in 2015, NASA, along with the National Additive Manufacturing Innovation Institute, launched a competition to design and 3D print a habitat for deep space exploration. More than 165 ideas were submitted, and the top thirty were judged on architectural concept, design approach, habitability, innovation, functionality, Mars site selection, and 3D print constructability, according to NASA. In September of that year, NASA awarded a total of $50,000 to first-, second-, and third-place teams. As of 2017, phase two of the $2.5 million competition was under way, and phase three was under development.

Team Space Exploration Architecture and Clouds Architecture Office won the first phase of the competition for their design, Mars Ice House. The team was awarded $25,000 at the 2015 World Maker Faire in New York. The name is not metaphorical: the team proposed 3D printing in ice. Inspired by NASA's "follow the water" approach to space exploration—that is, going where water is found, since water is necessary for human life—the winning team decided to use water as its primary building material. They did so for several reasons: water is a naturally occurring part of the environment where the habitat would be built; it allows astronauts to both interact with their new environment and be protected from it; and water works with the technology, 3D printing, being used.

Building a structure out of ice fits with the competition's requirement that the habitat be useful on Mars. It's predicted that astronauts will continue to find water on the planet, so the Mars Ice House "takes full advantage of [water's] properties as an indigenous material that acts … as a life-force to sustain a human and plant ecosystem."

The material and shape of the habitat also allow the structure to be above ground "to bring light to the interior and to create visual connections to the landscape beyond, allowing the mind as well as the body to thrive," according to the team's website, marsicehouse.com. The semitranslucent exterior of ice helps to blend the comfort of home with the newness of the Martian landscape, visually blurring the divide between interior and exterior.

An ice home would allow the astronauts stationed on Mars to live above ground. Living below ground would disrupt the astronauts' biological rhythms, keeping them always in darkness, a state of perpetual nighttime rather than the cycle of day and night. Also, the dangerous substances naturally occurring in Mars's soil could harm them. Danger lurks from above, in the form of solar radiation, but the ice would act as a barrier against that, filtering the sun's rays. Water both allows daylight through and absorbs high-energy, short-wavelength radiation.

Amazingly, using ice also works with the competition's requirement that the habitat be 3D printed.

Using ice as the extruded, or printed, material, is unusual but not unheard of. In 2012, *PC World* reported on two researchers at McGill University in Canada who printed with water and potassium chloride brine—a material that freezes at a lower temperature than water. The potassium chloride brine was used for support structures to hold up overhanging pieces of their models while they were being printed. At the end of the process, the model was put in a slightly warmer place and the brine melted away, leaving a sculpture of pure ice behind. The article suggested that "the most obvious purpose" for printing in ice would be to make drinking glasses; a frozen glass would be the ultimate way to keep a beverage chilled while a person enjoys it. But Team Space Exploration Architecture and Clouds Architecture Office has taken the application to a whole new level.

They are working on a bigger and more complex scale than glasses or sculptures, and they are working to place their printed object, an entire habitat, in an environment far more hostile and strange than an earthly wintry party or city festival, which is where most ice glasses or sculptures are used. They consulted with astrophysicists, geologists, structural engineers, and 3D printing experts to understand the temperature and pressure conditions of the Martian environment in conjunction with the physical deposition techniques they designed. They selected a process to turn ice into water vapor, which they used to deposit liquid water in an environment cold enough to print a form in solid ice. Bots named iBo used a triple nozzle to dispense a mixture of water, fiber, and aerogel in rings, layer upon layer. (Aerogel is a super-light synthetic material derived from gel, but the liquid component of the gel has been replaced by gas. To visualize it, think of it by one of its nicknames: frozen smoke.) It is "structurally sound, insulated and translucent," the winning team writes on its website.

In the next chapter we'll look at 3D printing domestic goods, as well as props and costumes used to imitate real-life objects for Hollywood movies. In many ways, to print them is not as massive an undertaking as printing a house—but the intricacies of design and the varieties of materials and objects make these fascinating places to find 3D design.

TECHNICAL TERMS

4D printing 4D printing adds "transformation" to 3D "length/width," "depth," and "height." Something that is 4D printed changes on its own into a different shape.

open-source project A project which has its computer code, instructions, or other details openly available for use and modification.

sparse fill A 3D printing technique that allows the printed object to appear solid from the outside but the inside is a grid like a honeycomb.

CHAPTER THREE

3D Printing in Everyday Life and on the Big Screen

W HILE 3D PRINTING HAS EXISTED IN PRACTICE FOR A good twenty years, its application has been limited for most of that time to industry, according to Daniel Burrus in a *Wired* article. But around the second decade of the twenty-first century, "rapid advances" in what Burrus calls "The Three Digital Accelerators" happened. Improvements in processing power, storage, and bandwidth encouraged a wide variety of not only smaller or niche business uses but also consumer uses. In this chapter, we explore two areas that are making surprising use of 3D technology: home or

Opposite: Creative executives of animation studio LAIKA and some of their creations attended a 2015 Oscars talk on stop-motion animation, including the role of 3D printing.

personal goods, and entertainment, specifically movies and museums.

3D Printing Home Art

In 2015, MIT took 3D printing to the next level by figuring out how to print in glass. Some of the most striking work in this medium with that technology came out of the university a year later, in the collection of death masks titled *Vespers*, an artistic exploration of the type of masks made in some cultures of a person's face after death.

Neri Oxman and the Mediated Matter Group at MIT Media Lab worked with Stratasys to produce these. According to *Creators*, Vice Media's arts and culture platform, they designed 3D models and then transformed those images into objects with high-resolution Stratasys Objet500 Connex3 Color Multi-Material 3D printers. "Our projects require us to invent computational design tools and technologies to create them," Oxman told *Creators*. "In that sense, the relationship between our design ambitions and the technologies that enable them is, well, 'non-platonic.' We look for design opportunities where the technique defines an expression as much as the expression defines the technique." The exhibition debuted at the London Design Museum.

This beautiful art was made possible by the foundational research done at MIT. People there developed a high-temperature system that could successfully melt glass so that it could work as a 3D

Neri Oxman's *Pneuma 2* is displayed in a 3D printing exhibition at the Science Museum in London.

printer's "ink," while maintaining the strength and clarity of glass. "The stream of glowing molten glass from the nozzle resembles honey," David Chandler writes for MIT News, "as it coils onto a platform, cooling and hardening as it goes."

Molten glass is loaded into a hopper in the top of the 3D printer. Everything, from the hopper to the nozzle through which the glass is extruded to the glass itself, must be kept heated to precise temperatures so the layers of molten glass stick to each other but don't smoosh together like melting ribbons of cake frosting. Everything needs to be hot–around 1,900 degrees Fahrenheit (1,038 degrees Celsius)–but requires some finesse. "Glass is inherently a very difficult material to work with," John Klein, one of the researchers, told MIT News. This, Chandler explains, is because glass's "viscosity changes with temperature, requiring precise control of temperature at all stages of the process." The researchers discovered that if

FDM, SPARSE FILL, AND 4D PRINTING

Fused deposition modeling (FDM) technology is the most common method of 3D printing, and it allowed for consumer desktop 3D printers to take off. It was invented by Stratasys, a 3D printer manufacturer founded in 1989. FDM follows three steps. First, preprocessing prepares a 3D CAD file. Next, in production, a 3D printer heats thermoplastic to a semiliquid state and deposits it in ultrafine beads. Finally, in postprocessing, the built object is removed from the supporting material used in the build.

Sparse fill in 3D printing means that from the outside, a printed object appears solid, but on the inside, it is a grid of open spaces, like a honeycomb. Using this technique can offer three advantages over solid fill. One, it can reduce a printed object's weight, cost, and build time. Two, if a maker tells the 3D printer to leave part of the printed object exposed, the sparse fill offers an interesting pattern; it can add to the object's aesthetics, or beauty. And three, designers and engineers can use sparse fill to manipulate the mechanical properties of an object. They can make certain sections denser than others. For example, the head of a hammer might be made denser than its handle. Shifting where the tool is balanced makes using the hammer less stressful on the wrist and arm. It also makes the striking part of the hammer, the neck and face, stronger.

4D printing adds "transformation" to 3D "length/width," "depth," and "height." Something that is 4D printed changes on its own into a different shape. For example, according to *iQ*, Intel's tech culture magazine, 4D-printed "skin" for skin grafts would change shape on its own after being applied to a person who has been seriously wounded or burned. It would grow with the person, not with more surgeries. Another example is a 4D-printed water pipe that could, on its own, adapt to changes in the environment; if the ground shifts, the pipe could contract or expand, as needed. It could even pulse to move water through itself.

they maintained three separate components along the "assembly line," they would succeed.

With this new capability, researchers are thinking about how to quickly produce everything from pieces of art to camera lenses and microprocessors. In 2017, German scientists began printing intricate glass objects only a few millimeters in size, with features as small as a few tens of micrometers (1 micrometer is equal to 0.001 millimeters, or 0.00004 inches). They manage this control of material with a special "liquid glass" they developed, which is a glass powder embedded into a liquid polymer. After the glassy object has been printed, it goes into a high-temperature oven. When melted together, the glass particles become a transparent sheet. Oxman wondered to *MIT News*, "Could we surpass the modern architectural tradition of discrete formal and functional partitions, and generate an all-in-one building skin that is at once structural and transparent?"

DIY 3DP

The 3D printing community is often a very open one, widely (and many times freely) sharing files, tips, ideas, and solutions. The Further Information section at the end of this book offers some places to find this community. These resources include step-by-step written and video tutorials on creating and 3D printing objects—in other words, do it yourself (DIY) 3D printing. Here are a couple of ideas to get you started.

Print Your Own Video Game Character

3DPrint.com, a news organization reporting on the 3D printing industry, offers a tutorial on printing World of Warcraft (WoW) characters. What's exciting about this is how simple it is—as long as you have access to a 3D printer and know how to use it. Thanks to **open-source projects** that offer 3D images of WoW characters and other programs that code it for you, you don't need to know design or G-code in order to print your very own rogue, warrior, or swift spectral tiger.

Following are the basic steps; the link to the full tutorial, including a short video, is in the Further Information section.

1. Download and familiarize yourself with the WoW model viewer program, an open-source project that allows people to view and download WoW characters.
2. Open the model viewer program (make sure to exit out of WoW before you do so, or this program won't work) and search for the character model you want.
3. Choose "File" once you've located your character, and scroll down to "Export Model." Choose "Object" from several other options.
4. Name and save this file somewhere easy to find, like your desktop.
5. Download MeshLab, an open-source program for preparing 3D images, specifically **triangular meshes**, for printing. (There are other programs also available, if you want to choose a different one and follow its instructions.)
6. Import your character file by going to "File" and scrolling to the "Import" choice.
7. Choose the file you want to import by clicking on it and then clicking "OK" in the pop-up box.
8. Go to "File" again and scroll down to choose "Export Mesh As."
9. Change the file to STL and save it again.
10. Turn your 3D printer on, open up your character STL file, and send it to the printer.

Design (and Then Print) Your Own Creation

A big part of the fun of 3D printing is making something you've designed, or at least drawn from someone else's design. Drawing with the goal of turning that drawing into a three-dimensional object is different than if your idea will stay a two-dimensional drawing on the page.

3D PRINTING TIP

After a 2015 *New Yorker* article about 3D printing cookie cutters, *Slate* reminded readers that complicated shapes don't often translate accurately during baking. Tested shapes of cutters are already available in stores. Plus, when it comes to making cookies, the point is the cookie, so bakers might do well to spend time and effort on improving the recipe, not the cutter.

Here are some basic things to remember to do, according to "8 Tips for 3D Printing with Sketchup," from MasterSketchup.com, an education site for users of the free 3D modeling site SketchUp.

1. Make your model watertight. Your 3D printer can't handle objects that have holes, gaps, or any openings. Imagine filling your object with water–if it would leak, it won't survive printing.
2. Make sure the sides, or walls, of your object are thick enough to not collapse in the real world. How thick is thick enough depends on the material you're using. Some plastics, for example,

require only a thin wall, less than 1 millimeter (0.04 inches), while ceramics require walls be at least 3 millimeters (0.1 inches) thick.

3. Scale up. If you make teeny features, smaller than one-sixteenth of an inch (1.6 millimeters), SketchUp may fail to read them—they are simply too small for the program. Scale up by a factor of one thousand (to simplify the math) for designing, and then scale down to what you want for printing.

4. SketchUp is a "polygonal surface modeling" program. This means that even curves are not smooth arcs but a series of flat surfaces. When drawing an arc or a circle, increase the number of segments used to make that curve so that each segment is about 1 millimeter long.

5. Understand your printer and the material you're using before you even start designing. The printer and the materials you feed it can only do what they physically can do.

6. Design for cost. 3D printing is nice because you only pay for what you use, and there are ways to lessen how much material you use. Make your walls as thin as they can be and use sparse fill rather than solid fill.

With these ideas in mind, consider drawing something of your own to then 3D print. Matt Donley, founder of MasterSketchup.com, started using SketchUp in 2007 with no instruction—he experimented and played until he figured it out and improved his skills. Now he's created, among other tutorials, a text and video guide to making a vase that can be 3D printed. The link to that is in the Further Information section of this book.

Printing Clothes

When Nervous System succeeded in 2014 at 3D printing a dress that was wearable, beautiful, and scientifically sound, the design studio helped 3D printing make a big leap forward. The Museum of Modern Art (MoMA) in New York City acquired it for its permanent collection.

Garments have been 3D printed before, but since the technology creates hard objects, the pieces of clothing were always too rigid to be truly wearable. While they were beautiful works of tech-filled art, they were difficult to move in and sit in. Nervous System used Kinematics, its unique 4D printing system, which was also acquired by MoMA, to create a dress that could be printed as one folded piece. Composed of thousands of hinged pieces, the dress was removed from the 3D printer looking like a lump of netting. Jessica Rosenkrantz and Jesse Louis-Rosenberg, Nervous System's founders and lead designers, along with the 3D print crew, shook the tangle, using their fingers to loosen the folds. They set the garment on a vibrating platform that further rattled the plastic pieces, shaped like petals and pie slices, to lie flat next to each other, forming a dress. Each piece is hard, but because of the thousands of "seams," the dress can move with the wearer, as a cloth dress would.

Nervous System's 3D-printed Kinematics Dress 1 moves like fabric.

Shapeways, the company that 3D printed the dress, interviewed Rosenkrantz about the process. She said that she and Louis-Rosenberg were "more interested in designing a process and material than a garment," testing 3D printing's benefits and shortcomings and creating a piece in solving the customizable wearables puzzle. They were looking at the bigger picture of revolutionizing fashion for consumers.

The designers created a 3D image of the dress and then, using mathematical formulas, digitally folded the dress so that it took up less space and the 3D printer could print it, as a "crumpled" ball, in one piece. Rosenkrantz credited her and Louis-Rosenberg's understanding of "the behavior of the geometry" for their ability to do this. Someone without an understanding of geometry might print many smaller panels that would have to be manually pieced together after they were printed. Rosenkrantz and Louis-Rosenberg "flipped the idea on its head … to take something very large and 3D and make it flatter and more compact, so it can be 3D printed in one piece."

DISSENTING VOICE

According to a 2017 *Shapeways Magazine* article, the Foodini wrongly claims to be a 3D printer of food; in actuality, it assembles food. Using hands alone, a person can't layer ropes of melted plastic into a functioning solid object. The ability to do that is what makes a 3D printer special. But hands alone can layer pasta with sauce and call it spaghetti. That's called assembling. Food printers, the industry magazine opines, can't really print. Extruding an edible ingredient into a layered item is creating exactly, and only, what a person using his or her hands could create.

Kinematics "is completely different from traditional modeling," Rosenkrantz told Shapeways, because "the whole system is built up around the logic of a mechanism, in this case a hinge, which has been optimized for 3D printing and whose behavior we can simulate." This was a new alternative to previous experiments that required the 3D printer to print a laid-out dress in pieces that needed to be adhered into one garment.

The Shapeways 3D printing engineers worked closely with Rosenkrantz and Louis-Rosenberg throughout the design process, confirming that the dress was being designed to printer specifications. This was such a complex project that they couldn't afford to try it a second time. They had to be perfect the first time. It took forty-four hours to print and finalize one dress.

Printed Fashion Pioneers

Rosenkrantz credited Jiri Evenhuis and Janne Kyttanen with inspiring Nervous System's fashion sensibilities. According to *Additive Fashion* online magazine, as of 2013, there had been thirteen known 3D-printed outfits. A dress by Evenhuis and Kyttanen was the first, 3D printed in 2000.

In the late 1990s, Evenhuis and Kyttanen were working as industrial engineers in the Netherlands. Together, they developed a printable fabric and then the first printed dress, named the Drape Dress. MoMA acquired it more than a decade before it bought Nervous System's next-generation dress. Kyttanen founded Freedom of Creation, a 3D printing research and design firm that would be later bought by 3D Systems. Its 2005 White Dress is now housed at the museum of the Fashion Institute of Technology.

Issey Miyake's famous "folding clothes" are a cloth inspiration for these 3D printed dresses, and this designer also uses 3D printing sometimes. According to a Clicklab video posted to YouTube, the garments are designed in a computer software program, which "generates intricate three-dimensional shapes from a

NEW TECHNOLOGY FOR AN OLD TRADITION

Fields such as medicine, science, and transportation seem to be natural places to use 3D printing because doctors, scientists, and researchers have always used

technology and are constantly striving for new solutions to complicated problems. Weddings, built on tradition, seem like one of the last places that such advanced technology would be useful, but

These wax models of engagement rings were 3D printed. This saves money and adds a personal touch to the rings.

people are finding that 3D printing has a role there, too: in making engagement rings.

Engagement rings may be 3D printed in wax and then cast in metal, including gold and platinum. PLA, or polylactic acid, is a biodegradable plastic derived from renewable resources, such as corn starch, tapioca roots, or sugarcane. It is a common material used in 3D printing, and now that materials such as metal powder can be added to PLA, it can make an attractive ring, no casting required.

There are a few reasons a person might choose to make an engagement ring rather than buy it. This allows the person to have a say in the design, be creative, and include personalized details. It can lower the cost significantly. Nghia Vuong, who designed and 3D printed a ring for his girlfriend, says in his *Medium* report on the project that if he bought the same ring in a store, it would cost 40 to 60 percent more. Making a ring requires more time, effort, and skill than choosing one from a store, but it also provides a unique story for the wearer and the giver!

single flat sheet of paper." Miyaki's team replicates the forms in recycled PET polyester, which is creased in traditional origami patterns. Garments "lie folded flat like a series of collapsed geometric landscapes. Pulled up and unfolded, however, each compressed form gracefully spatialize[s] into three dimensions."

3D-Printed Footwear

Tech expert Daniel Burrus wrote in 2014 about 3D printing shoes as an "enticing" idea for a few reasons.

One, the current shoe-sizing system does not account for the width of feet. Shoe sizes such as 6 or 8.5 refer only to length, so people with wider or narrower feet than what is considered by the industry to be standard have a hard time finding shoes that fit well.

Current shoe sizing also makes both shoes in a pair identical in size and shape, but few people have feet that are perfect mirror images of each other. If all shoes were 3D printed, photographs would be taken of a customer's feet, and a 3D image would be created from those photographs, which would be adjusted with further data about the customer's height, weight, and activities while wearing the shoes.

Feetz is an example of a company already putting this into practice. In 2016, the US company finished its first one hundred pairs of shoes, each custom fit from information submitted via the customer's smartphone and entirely 3D printed, sole to toe. Reviewer Sarah Anderson Goehrke of 3DPrint.com test-drove a pair, noting first how "*viable*" (her emphasis) these shoes seemed as useful, wearable footwear. They were both sturdy and flexible; there was an arch; and the print lines, which would give away that these shoes had been made by layering material extruded by a printer, were barely visible.

New Balance and Adidas have also been working to make sporty 3D-printed shoes for the masses. Adidas announced plans to encourage customers to order the shoe in-store and then, later, test the prototype out on a store treadmill. That way an employee could see how the customer moved not in general but in those exact shoes, so the rest of the shoe could be finished with the customer's running or walking specifications in mind.

Burrus's second reason for liking the idea of 3D-printed shoes is that the technology can help people in extreme situations. SOLS Systems, he wrote in 2014, has started using 3D printing to improve its design and manufacturing of orthotic shoes, or footwear for people with chronic pain or injured feet. The main purpose of these shoes is to help a person who needs more support than standard shoes provide. Customized shoes that are also affordable and quickly made will revolutionize the field. Orthotic shoes are also not known for being fashion forward, but this technology could help shoemakers create stylish shoes that also provide support.

Athletes also require specialized shoes, and 3D printing can improve the performance of their shoes. Nike has combined 3D knitting and 3D shoe printing into a football cleat that is exactly tailored to each foot of each athlete, making it rather like a second skin. Nike used the same 3D knitting technology, its own Flyknit, when it made a shoe for gold medal–winning American sprinter Allyson Felix. A variety of data points, supplied by the shoe designers and engineers as well as Felix and her coaches, were plugged into the design software. Felix met with the Nike team more than twelve times. Thirty versions of the shoe's spiky plate were produced, and the shoe's upper was adjusted more than seventy times. "The product that has been created is making [Felix] measurably better," Tony Bignell, Nike's vice president of footwear innovation, said in an interview.

In 2015, in a blend of fashion and athleticism, gold medal–winning British skeleton racer Amy Williams wore a pair of 3D-printed shoes that combined form

Amy Williams, an athlete and television show presenter, has tested 3D-printed shoes that blend function and beauty.

with function. As a presenter on *The Gadget Show*, a British television program about consumer technology, she participated in a feature on future fashion. Designer Julian Hakes, who has been focusing on 3D-printed footwear, worked with prototype manufacturer Ogle to produce a wearable high heel that has a 3D printed gold nylon heel. The top is woven leather pieces, which also shows how, according to 3DPrint.com, "conventional techniques and materials can work with the technology in a complementary fashion."

3D Printing and Hollywood

Iron Man's suit. The spider in the second part of *Harry Potter and the Deathly Hallows*. As far back as these movies, released early in the second decade of the twenty-first century, big-budget Hollywood productions have been using 3D printing. In his live-action scenes in *Iron Man 2*, Robert Downey Jr. wore a suit that was digitally modeled and then 3D printed, before it was painted to look metallic. In the final Harry Potter movie, the smaller version of the giant spider was 3D printed.

Jason Lopes, a system engineer with Legacy Effects, a special effects studio, told CNET that Hollywood is increasingly using 3D printing. It's an efficient way to create complex costumes, especially in the draft stages, when a company such as Legacy Effects is still determining what a client wants. Instead of crafting new foam models by hand at each stage of development, designers can quickly design and print a small version of the object, show the clients, and move forward.

What's really exciting is that because 3D-printed objects are made from the same 3D images that are used to create computer-generated images (CGI), the props or costumes used for live-action scenes will look like their CGI versions.

Other designers, like Mark Coulier of Coulier Creatures, agree that 3D printing offers a lot of benefits, like speed, but they still prefer hand-sculpting. "You get what I call happy accidents when you sculpt things physically with a clay material that just don't happen when you sculpt on the computer," he told *Live Science*.

Hollywood uses 3D printers that are much more expensive than home models. According to CNET, they can cost tens of thousands of dollars—and the quality of their work makes the high price tag worth it. If you look closely at objects printed on most home 3D printers, you can see the fine layer lines. There are no such lines visible

The suit that Robert Downey Jr. wore for his title role in *Iron Man 2* was 3D printed to fit him exactly.

with the high-quality machines, which print in layers only 16 microns thick: the width of one-third of a human hair.

Museum-Quality Replica

For the 2012 exhibition *Slavery at Jefferson's Monticello: Paradox of Liberty*, curators at the National Museum of American History, a part of the Smithsonian, needed a statue of Thomas Jefferson. A life-size bronze statue at Monticello, Jefferson's home in Virginia, would have been perfect but couldn't be moved. Making a copy of that statue with traditional methods, rubber molding and casting, would have taken several months. The Smithsonian curators wanted an option that maintained the quality but sped up the time. They turned to 3D printing.

The Smithsonian's Digitization Program Office took 3D laser scans of the Monticello statue. RedEye On Demand took that digital model and made a figure from it. It used FDM technology, printing the statue in four pieces (which were later pieced together with pegs) with production-grade thermoplastics. Because the engineers used a sparse fill technique, the statue's interior looked like a honeycomb. This material, thermoplastics, plus the structure, the honeycomb, meant the statue was lighter and less expensive than traditional statues but also strong and durable. Primer, paint, and wax gave the figure a bronze look. Building the statute took four hundred hours, the equivalent of two and a half weeks.

This successful use of 3D printing to make a statue worthy of the United States' premier museum was exciting for the curators of this exhibition, and it also promised more useful collaborations. According to CNET, as of 2012, only about 2 percent of the Smithsonian's collection was available to visitors. Having the ability to make digital 3D models means there doesn't have to be physical space to display items, and people can view them from homes and schools around the world, not just in person at the Smithsonian. Physical 3D-printed models can be housed in more than one museum and also can be touched and studied more in-depth than delicate original artifacts can be.

Health care takes 3D printing for preservation and education to the next level—turning its output into life-improving, sometimes even life-saving, products, devices, and even body parts. The next chapter looks at that.

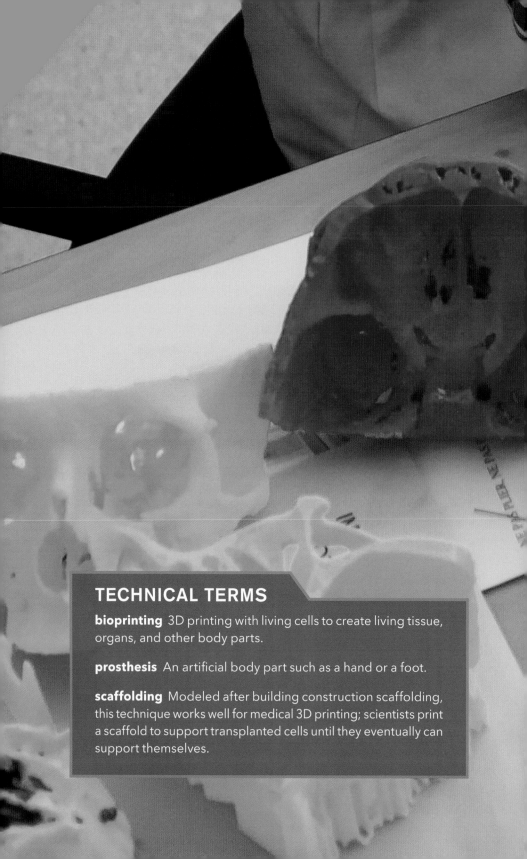

TECHNICAL TERMS

bioprinting 3D printing with living cells to create living tissue, organs, and other body parts.

prosthesis An artificial body part such as a hand or a foot.

scaffolding Modeled after building construction scaffolding, this technique works well for medical 3D printing; scientists print a scaffold to support transplanted cells until they eventually can support themselves.

CHAPTER FOUR

3D Printing in Health Care

THE OUTLOOK FOR MEDICAL USE OF 3D PRINTING IS evolving at an extremely rapid pace as specialists are beginning to use 3D printing in more advanced ways. One of the most revolutionary of these is using 3D printing to educate people about their own health, medical conditions, and treatment options, giving them more access to information and opportunities to take control of their own health. Just as the section on math in 3D printing, in chapter 1, showed how 3D printing could help students see complex shapes and the mathematical formulas behind them, in medicine, doctors are printing 3D models of their patients' body parts in order to help

Opposite: These 3D-printed sections of a facial skeleton, made from medical imaging, allow for custom implants.

them better understand what's happening in their own bodies. For example, according to a story from KHOU, a news outlet out of Houston, Texas, neurosurgeon David Baskin 3D prints models of his patients' brains to show them where a tumor is or how their brain is ridged with Alzheimer's. This helps patients and doctors alike choose among and prepare for treatments. Prakash Masand, the division chief of cardiac imaging in the department of radiology at Texas Children's Hospital, also sees the benefit of a 3D-printed model because "you can look at all the angles."

The following stories share some of the incredible 3D printing applications in health care, from **prostheses** to medical devices. Some of this work is so accessible that high school and college students are using it to make a big impact in their communities.

College Students 3D Print Prosthetic Hands

College students don't yet have the formal schooling necessary to allow them to fully participate in **bioprinting**, but that hasn't stopped some in Cincinnati, Ohio, from doing a world of good with 3D printing.

Enable UC is an organization that 3D prints prosthetic hands for kids—and it was founded by biomedical engineering students at the University of Cincinnati (UC). According to an article printed in USA Today, as of early 2017, they had made forty-two hands

Enable UC members stand with the first recipient of one of their 3D-printed hands.

and other assistive devices and given them free of charge to people like thirteen-year-old Brody. He was the first person to receive an Enable UC hand, and the students set the bar high with this first project. Brody was born with a partial right hand, but now this Star Wars movie buff has a full hand that looks like a stormtrooper's hand.

UC students follow a process that takes them from meeting a patient to fitting that person with a new hand. They receive a photo of a patient's arm that needs the prosthesis. Then they search e-Nable's open-source 3D design files for hands or fingers that will suit that particular patient. E-Nable is an international organization that also provides free prosthetic hands to kids; it directly inspired UC students to take similar action. After the UC students have customized the design, they send it to the 3D printer. Twelve to twenty-four hours later, the students have a collection of printed parts, which they then piece together into a functioning hand.

Perhaps Enable UC's most unique case involves them working with a seven-year-old girl to help her deal with a nerve injury in her arm. She's not missing an arm, hand, or fingers, but she can't use the ones she has—her fingers won't close, so she can't pick anything up. The college students are building her the first-ever brachial plexus arm. It will include a glove design to help her hold on to objects. They hope their work will change yet another life.

Enable UC isn't trying to replace the professional work of trained doctors and engineers. These hands don't include robotics or electric sensors. They're wholly 3D-printed plastic, so they can stay affordable (each costing the university less than twenty dollars to make) and so the students and their patients can have a little bit of fun with the shape. But make no mistake about it: even the craziest of 3D-printed hands is functional. For the first time in their lives, these young patients can shake hands, catch a ball, ride a bike with two hands on the handlebars, hold a glass, open a bottle of nail polish, or play the violin. Perhaps someday these kids will get more sophisticated prosthetic hands, but the Enable UC hands are a great start, especially considering a professionally made hand can cost $6,000 to $10,000.

Printing for a Community

A request by a community member started a group of Houston, Texas, high school students on a path to helping others with their 3D printer. Kaedon Olsen was born

ALL BODIES CAN BE PERFECT

A person missing a body part or with a malfunctioning body part does not have to get a new one. In this chapter's story about high school students printing one for Kaedon Olsen, his mother was quick to say that she had wanted to leave the decision to get a prosthesis or not to him. News outlet KHOU paraphrased her explanation: "It's his body after all."

without some fingers due to a genetic condition. After his mother heard about 3D printing technology on the news, she asked her area high school, which she knew had a 3D printer, if they could help her son. The computer science teacher thought it was a great idea and, according to local news outlet KHOU, led his students through an online search for guidance in how to do this. These Brenham High School students found e-Nable, the same organization the University of Cincinnati students worked with. Two months later, Kaedon had a new hand.

"The moment that we gave it to him and we realized this isn't just a project, this is somebody's life and opening up possibilities for them," teacher Trenton Hall told KHOU, "that was life-changing for us as well."

Washington University students fit a ten-year-old with a 3D-printed robotic prosthesis.

Nine-year-old Ja'Lea Henderson, born without a fully formed right hand, also benefited from the class's 3D printing skills. Just as Kaedon's mom had expressed that she didn't want to force her son to get a prosthetic hand—he was a fully functioning human being the way he was born—so Ja'Lea was also a whole person without making her hand conform to standards of "normalcy." According to KHOU, she could dress herself and tie her shoes; she was even a cheerleader and dancer, and had a great mental outlook, so she did well in school. Still, her new pink-and-purple arm has helped her perform even better in school. For example, her handwriting and typing have improved.

"Ovary of the Future"

In May 2017, researchers announced that they'd found "the holy grail of bioengineering for regenerative medicine": they had 3D printed working mouse ovaries, the part of the female body that produces eggs. Teresa Woodruff led this team of researchers from Northwestern University Feinberg School of Medicine and McCormick School of Engineering, outside of Chicago. Though this technology had been tested only on mice as of the summer of 2017, Woodruff said in a video interview with *Northwestern Now* that the ultimate goal of it is to restore reproductive health and function in young women. Diseases such as cancer can ruin the ability of some people to have biological children.

Woodruff explained how important this was in an interview with National Public Radio's *Morning Edition*. She and her team found something for which they'd been searching for a long time, something precious, a really big deal—in this case, a technology that would catapult medicine far forward. Bioengineering is the replacement of damaged or missing body parts with artificial ones, and regenerative medicine refers to creating living replacements. By 3D printing ovaries in the manner they developed, Woodruff and her colleagues were doing all this: using artificial as well as healthy organic materials to create from scratch an entirely new organ, a bioprosthesis, that would function just as a naturally occurring ovary would—better, of course, in the case of a patient needing a new organ.

Biological 3D printing is similar to playing with Lincoln Logs, Alexandra Rutz, a member of the team that 3D printed mouse ovaries, explained in an interview with

Northwestern Now. As you place the wooden or plastic toy logs on top of one another, you build a cabin, but each time you play, your cabin can look different from the last time. If you shorten the distance between logs, you may form a window; if you widen it, you may form a door.

3D PRINTING TIP

If you are 3D printing something complex or with a sensitive purpose, you don't want to go it alone. The team that 3D printed working mouse ovaries found both much-needed inspiration and humor in working collaboratively. It was "motivational" that the team working on female health issues was made up entirely of female researchers. Together, they could joke about being the mouse babies' grandparents.

In biological 3D printing, the "logs" are called "filaments," and the distance and angle between them can also be adjusted. The space between filaments forms not windows and doors but pores, tiny openings in which healthy tissue is placed to give that tissue a safe space to naturally function on its own. And by experimenting with where those filament "logs" are placed, Rutz said, researchers can make different sizes of pores and different types of groupings of pores. This arrangement affects how well the ovary functions, or doesn't, in the case of her research field. There needs to be structure in order to protect the tissue but also room "for the egg cells to mature and ovulate, as well as blood vessels to form within the implant enabling the hormones to circulate within the mouse bloodstream and trigger lactation after giving birth."

Just like you would 3D print a plastic toy at home, extruding layer upon layer of plastic, building the structure up until it forms the toy, the scientists at Northwestern extruded layer upon layer of their material, referred to as "a biological ink." The "ink" they used was gelatin. Gelatin comes from collagen, which naturally occurs in many places in the body, so it's a safe substance. Its composition also strikes the perfect balance of being strong enough to be handled during surgery, when the new ovary is transplanted into the patient, and being porous enough to work with the patient's body, accepting blood flow, for example.

Researchers in Germany, at the Fraunhofer Institute for Interfacial Engineering and Biotechnology, started experimenting with 3D printing with gelatin in 2013, according to Engineering.com. They devised a way to keep the normally jellylike substance in liquid form, like ink, during the printing and then cure it with a UV light, making it solid. At the time, the researchers were still struggling to get that printed object to support the body in functioning naturally. "Only once we are successful in producing tissue that can be nourished through a system of blood vessels can printing larger tissue structures become feasible," Kirsten Borcher, one of the researchers there, told Engineering.com. Therefore, the engineering news site concluded, "3D printed organs are still a long way off."

This scaffold for a bioprosthetic mouse ovary was 3D printed in gelatin.

An amazingly short four years later, the Northwestern University team was making that a reality. The printed gelatin formed a structure about the size of a pea but complex in form, including even microscopic pores. That was the bioengineering part. Next, the researchers incorporated naturally created materials, placing real tissue from mouse ovaries into the 3D printed ovary form. This tissue, the follicles, contains immature eggs and cells that secrete, or give off, hormones needed for reproduction.

Woodruff and her team then had homemade— lab-made—mouse ovaries. They transplanted them into mice. Three of the seven mice gave birth to two babies each. Ramille Shah, a member of Woodruff's team, told *Northwestern Now* that one of the things they learned from this was that the structure holding the follicles mattered—it was key to the new ovary's success. "We wouldn't be able to do that if we didn't use a 3-D printer platform," Shah said.

It's important to note that the researchers refer to the structure they 3D printed as a scaffold. In a video interview with *Northwestern Now*, Monica Laronda encouraged viewers to think of a common example of **scaffolding**: the structure of tubes and platforms set up first during the construction of a building. This network, mimicking the building being formed inside the scaffold's perimeter, supports the builders by giving them a safe place to work and hold their materials and other supplies, but the scaffolding isn't meant to last; it will be removed as the building takes its own solid form. By erecting a scaffold first, Laronda explained, "they're building something that will eventually support itself." That's exactly what these researchers are trying to do for reproductive organs. *Northwestern Now* reported they wanted to build something that not only functions as it is but also is "successful in boosting hormone production and restoring fertility" for the body's long-term self-sustaining health.

Researchers plan to continue to experiment to find the most successful scaffolding form for ovaries. This process will also help researchers working in the replacement of other soft-tissue organs. According to an Engineering.com report from 2013, surveys conducted by the German Organ Transplantation Foundation found that the number of organ transplant donors was 18 percent lower compared to the previous year. If we could 3D print organs, we'd never be at risk of experiencing a shortage.

Striking a Nerve

According to the University of Minnesota, more than two hundred thousand people experience nerve damage from injury or disease each year. And because nerve regeneration, regrowing nerve function, is complex, it rarely happens. In other words, this is one area the body and medical science cannot usually correct. But as of 2015, a 3D printing technique developed by the University of Minnesota (along with collaborating institutions Virginia Tech, University of Maryland, Princeton University, and Johns Hopkins University) may help those people.

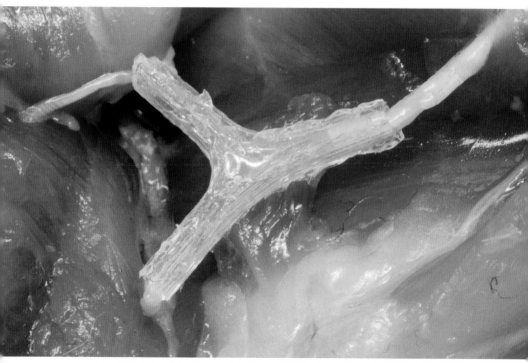

Scientists 3D printed a model of a rat's sciatic nerve, allowing the animal to regain mobility.

Researchers used 3D imaging and 3D printing techniques to create "a custom silicone guide implanted with biochemical cues to help nerve regeneration," according to a press release out of the University of Minnesota's College of Science and Engineering. This guide, or sleeve that mimics the damaged nerve, was tested on rats. It seemed to help regrow both the sensory and motor (controls movement) nerves.

First, researchers used a 3D scanner to reverse engineer the structure of a rat's sciatic nerve, the nerve that runs from the lower back to the feet. When that nerve is damaged or destroyed, walking is impaired or impossible. Of course, had the rat been a human patient coming into the hospital immediately after an injury, there would be no healthy nerve for the doctors to scan for creating a 3D image. So, according to *Inverse*, researchers would like to see a database of nerve images developed. Doctors could then search it, like looking through a catalog, for the nerve that best fits each patient.

Second, from the mouse's image, they 3D printed a silicone tube. They made sure there were microgrooves on the inner surface and biochemical cues embedded to encourage the artificial nerve to imitate a natural one. It could then trigger regrowth of a natural nerve.

The scientists then surgically implanted the silicone guide into the rat, grafting it to the cut ends of the nerve. Scanning and printing took about an hour. Within ten to twelve weeks, the rat could walk again.

Even Cooler Body Parts

Within medical applications, perhaps the most common use of 3D printing is to make prostheses, artificial body parts to replace missing natural parts or those so damaged they cannot be repaired. You may be able to imagine the war hero returning home, the survivor of a car accident, or the diabetic patient needing a replacement body part. Those limbs of metal, plastic, springs, and sometimes robotics have to be manufactured. Some are made by 3D printing.

3D-Printed Jaw

A woman made news in 2012 when she became the recipient of the first-ever 3D-printed jaw. This was incredible because it was unusual, so it demonstrated that hospitals could consider the possibility of "patient-specific" body implants.

It's also quite amazing in its own right. LayerWise, a company out of Belgium, made the complex shape out of one piece. It printed layers of titanium powder and then melted them together with a laser beam. The layers were incredibly thin—thirty-three layers stood only 1 millimeter (0.04 inches) tall—so the jaw was composed of thousands of layers, said Ruben Wauthle, LayerWise's medical applications engineer. The jaw was then coated with a bioceramic. It's porous to promote muscle and nerve attachment.

Suffering from osteomyelitis, a bone infection, the woman couldn't speak or swallow properly with her original jaw. After the transplant, she recovered full ability.

Magic Arms

In 2009, toddler Emma Lavelle received "magic arms," as she called them, an entire 3D printed exoskeleton that transformed her from a little girl who couldn't move to one who can play with her friends.

Emma was born with her body contorted so her legs were by her ears and her shoulders rotated inward. For her first two years of life, she was mostly in surgery or in casts to straighten her body out. Even once she could stand and walk on her own, however, the condition she was born with, arthrogryposis multiplex congenita, continued to prevent her from moving with full range of motion. This rare neuromuscular condition made her muscles so weak that she couldn't lift even a crayon.

The Center for Orthopedics Research and Development at Delaware's Nemours/Alfred I. duPont Hospital for Children had a solution—sort of. The Wilmington Robotic Exoskelton (WREX) is a body-powered upper-limb orthosis generally mounted to a wheelchair. It had been used successfully for a few years, but it was too big and heavy for such a little and, ideally, active person. The researchers came up with a workaround. Emma became the first child to be fitted with a 3D-printed version; by 2012, after she'd been using her magic arms for about three years, fifteen other kids had also been fitted with one, and a Magic Arms nonprofit now exists with the mission of helping get this device to all kids who need it. "Without the 3D printer, we would not be in a position we're in with these younger kids," Tariq Rahman, a mechanical engineer and head of pediatric engineering and research at Nemours, said in an interview. "I think 3D scanning and printing is the future for this field."

The plastic is the same kind of plastic that is used for Legos, so it's "human friendly," and it's also durable.

When not in competition, triathlete Sarah Reinersten wears a fairing, a 3D-printed cover for her prosthetic leg.

But if a piece does break, Emma's mom can send the design engineer a photo, and he can print a new one; the turnaround time is super fast.

"This is one of those industries that matches perfectly with 3D printing ... because we need custom everything," Whitney Sample, a research design engineer assigned to Emma, said.

3D-Printed Accessories for Prostheses

Prosthetic limbs are very cool in function, but they can look nonhuman. They might appear cold and foreign, a robot's limb looking strange on a human body. They might be seen as more like a part from an SUV on a Ferrari. Sarah Reinersten, interviewed for a 2011 CNET article, had her left leg amputated above the knee when she was seven because of a medical condition. For nearly thirty years, the triathlete lived with prostheses that were basically "a foam leg with a flesh-tone stocking."

Bespoke Innovations agreed that that was a pretty dismal standard. Founded by an industrial designer and an orthopedist, the company makes fairings, one-of-a-kind 3D-printed covers for prosthetic legs. It's more accurate to think of these covers as tattoos, however. At several thousand dollars each, they're not coming off. The technology allows the company to create lightweight but sturdy designs that also say something about the wearer's personality.

First, the company scans the client's body with two cameras to record details about shape and contour.

The system "does a whole lot of trigonometry and then meshes" the photos together into the 3D digital image. Then, artistry follows math, and the designers must take into account the physical attributes of the person and his or her age and personality in order to design the perfect new "skin."

While a fairing could be completed in one to three workdays, the process usually takes much longer while the client and the team discuss ideas.

Bespoke's founding designer, Scott Summit, has found this really appeals to returning military personnel. Fairings take "prosthetics from being generic and utilitarian into something cool as hell, and that really works for a soldier." Fortunately, the US military has been "supportive of some soldiers' wish" to get one, according to the CNET story.

Summit's team 3D prints fairings in any number of styles, abstract to concrete. Sometimes clients get ideas from architecture, movies, or even their favorite car part. Reinersten's fairing, shaped like her other leg, has a see-through herringbone design at the back. She told CNET that the design helps her "be part of a cultural shift that changes your idea of what is beautiful as we rebuild the human body in the modern world."

3D Printing Medical Supplies

Not all advancements in medical 3D printing are at the bioprinting level. Using 3D printing to make tools to be used in health care is a great way to keep some costs down. This is critical in parts of the world that are low on financial resources and to society in general as overall health care costs rise and people live longer than ever before.

3D Printing Tools

In 2014, Michigan Technological University published a library of open-source designs for a syringe pump. Anyone is free to access these instructions to manufacture syringe pumps, which are used for delivering precise amounts of liquid, such as medicine. People can even customize the instructions to make them fit their unique needs.

This matters because making your own syringe pump decreases the cost by a lot. In 2014, the devices sold for $250 to $2,500 each, but according to Joshua Pearce, an associate professor who led his students in creating this library of designs, making one costs $50. This is good not only for doctors helping patients but for researchers running experiments. Megan Frost, a colleague of Pearce's at Michigan Tech, told Engineering.com that the work of Pearce's team has really helped her biomedical engineering team. "We'd always wanted to run experiments concurrently, but we couldn't because the syringe pumps cost so much. This has really opened doors for us," she said.

And if Frost wanted to keep her experiments going while she was out of the lab, she could do that too, thanks to Pearce's team. They added to the design the option to use an inexpensive credit card–sized Raspberry Pi computer as a wireless controller. "That way, you can link the syringe pump to the network, sit on a beach in Hawaii and control your lab," Pearce told Engineering.com.

3D Printing Medicine

Chemistry is all about reaction—different chemicals reacting to each other and to outside influences. Pharmaceuticals, drugs used as medicine, are the products of chemical reactions. So, reactionware is an appropriate name for one of the most interesting uses of 3D technology: the printing of drugs.

In 2012, CNET reported that researchers at the University of Glasgow in Scotland were able to build drugs with a $2,000 commercial 3D printer. Interestingly, the printer is not "just" the printer but also the vessel for the drug. Using a robotically controlled syringe, the team mixed its chemicals not in glassware but with the printer itself. Because the vessel is part of the reaction process, "it gives us very specific control over reactions because we can continually refine the design of our vessels as required," Lee Cronin, head of the research team, said in a press release sent to CNET.

Cronin likened the process to making a layer cake: his team printed the last reactionary agent first and then built other chemical layers above it. The liquid that tops the entire stack seeps down to mix in different ways with each unique chemical layer.

Cronin liked the idea of 3D printing drugs for a few reasons, including accessibility. Within twenty years, he anticipated that the cost of printers and software would be low enough that drug-printing printers could be in developing countries. Eventually, he said, with "carefully-controlled software 'apps,'" anyone with access to a 3D printer, even if they weren't a medical professional, could print needed medication quickly, conveniently, and for less money.

3D printing is useful for all stages of care of the human body. In the next chapter, we look at using the technology to study the remains of those who have died from disease or been victims of violent crimes or accidents. By doing so, researchers hope to learn how to prevent or treat diseases and improve the justice process.

TECHNICAL TERMS

bioarchaeologist Someone who studies human remains from archaeological sites.

skull photographic superimposition A forensics technique used in conjunction with 3D printing; researchers compare recovered human remains with photographs of people who have gone missing to determine identity.

Virtopsy A trademarked term for a virtual autopsy that uses CT scans and 3D printed objects.

CHAPTER FIVE

3D Printing in Forensics and Other Careers

I N 2013, JOSHUA PEARCE OF MICHIGAN TECH AND HIS STUDENTS worked on 3D printing syringe pumps, as we learned in the last chapter. They developed an open-source 3D printer that prints in metal. Compared to the $250,000 price tag for metal 3D printers in 2016, the $1,500 cost of the Pearce team's printer was affordable. According to the press release about it, it could successfully print small metal sprockets. However, most people don't think about sprockets when they think of printing metal—they think of guns.

It would be strange not to mention guns in a book on the applications of 3D printing. When new technology

Opposite: Surgeons reference a 3D-printed model of an organ before proceding with an operation at Nagoya University Hospital in Japan. The model was printed off of a CT scan.

comes on the scene, it is easy, and understandable, to think about all the negative ways it could be used. Every other technology invented has been used for both benefit and harm, and 3D printing will likely be no different. The first 3D-printed metal gun, created by Solid Concepts (no longer in the gun business), was released in 2013. It could fire at least fifty rounds of ammunition without fault and proved, many experts said, how sturdy 3D-printed objects could be.

Three years later, 3DPrint.com was still saying the public had little to fear about technology being able to 3D print guns. The online magazine suggested that plastic was too flimsy to be useful for the complexity of guns. Guns made from a metal-plastic hybrid might be stronger, but they'd set off security alarms, and all-metal guns, like the Solid Concepts one, cost about $11,000. If someone wanted a gun, they'd wisely go with a traditionally made one. The magazine *Kids, Code, and Computer Science* agreed, saying that while guns can be 3D printed, there are many reasons a person wouldn't bother. "It's easier and safer to create a light saber."

As technology improves and becomes cheaper, it's probably a good idea for law enforcement to monitor the 3D-printed gun sector. In the meantime, people are already using 3D printing to great effect in a field that sometimes involves guns. Talking about printing weapons is a good transition into the usefulness of 3D printing in the field of forensics.

METAL METHODS

Printing with metal may follow one of three methods, according to Pinshape. In metal binder jetting, metal powder and a glue-like substance are printed in alternating layers, slowly building an object that, when dry, appears to be solid metal. After the object is cured, in this case heated in an oven for twenty-four hours, it can be filled with something like bronze filler.

Powder bed fusion also uses metal powder but not glue—instead, a high-temperature laser beam strikes the powder, fusing the granules into a solid.

Directed energy deposition is like powder bed fusion except it can extrude powder and then solidify it with heat or it can extrude metal wire to be fused with heat.

3D Printing and Forensics

Small-scale physical models of crime scenes have long been submitted into evidence during court cases to help jurors visualize where and how a crime might have happened. In a 2013 article, *Forensic Magazine* pointed out that recent advancements in 3D technology–from increased types of usable materials to lowered costs–are creating new ways for modeling to help those involved in the investigation of crime and the prosecution of criminals. These include the small and detailed, such as creating a model of a suspect's jaw and teeth to see how well a bite mark on a victim aligns with that dentition, and the large and complex, such as printing a model of a bombed building.

Accident Reconstruction

The reconstruction of car crashes and industrial accidents, among other events, using 3D printing allows for the examination of a wider variety of more complex settings. Data from police laser scanners can be used to create 3D models of complicated car crash scenes as well as each vehicle involved, showing the detailed collision patterns in their crushed metal. Replicas of cars can be physically moved to show how they started and how they fit together during the crash.

Similar to vehicle accident reconstruction, industrial accidents can be complex and too large to easily understand without modeling. Analysis of 3D-printed models of construction site incidents, for example, can provide clues about the failure of an important structural component. *Forensic Magazine* wrote of one investigation that used 3D printing to understand the failure of a construction crane. The investigators printed models of the crane and the building affected by its fall and placed them in a wind tunnel to understand how much of the accident was caused by the strong winds that day and how much must have been caused by something else, perhaps human error.

Footprints

Materials such as dental stone and Mikrosil have allowed investigators to create replicas of footprints and detailed, even microscopic, marks, such as those made by tools scraping bone. By doing so, investigators can preserve clues—for example, turning muddy footprints at a crime scene into sturdy stone that can be brought back to the lab. They can also study more closely marks not easily

Crime scene investigators use 3D printing technology in many ways. They can re-create footprints from digital images.

If there is anything in nature that might be 3D printed to help a criminal or accident investigation, it is best to take digital images of it before anyone attempts to examine the evidence. If any evidence is altered or damaged by conditions or handling, 3D prints can be made off of digital images so the evidence can be seen in its original state.

seen when left on the victim—making a cast of a gouge in a bone can help to highlight it. The idea is old and time tested, and 3D printing has improved upon it.

While the materials used to make casts always act as they should, the conditions that investigators use them in don't always work in an investigator's favor. That footprint on the sandy incline of a hillside may easily shift or even entirely crumble when an investigator pours dental powder mixed with water into the print to capture its shape in a cast. Time also plays a role. As *Forensic Magazine* reported, in remote areas, the first professionals to the scene of a crime may have little more than a digital camera handy. If they can't make a physical cast of the evidence immediately at the scene, 3D printing allows them to turn their photographs into models later.

Facial Reconstruction and Identification

There are ways in which 3D printing can help in identifying and studying human remains. **Skull photographic superimposition** allows investigators to compare a 3D-printed skull of an unidentified victim to a photograph of a missing person to see if the facial features match. This method can help in determining the identity of the person whose remains were found.

Printing a skeleton can also help in studying remains. For example, the long-buried remains of Richard III, the last English king to die in battle, were found beneath a parking lot in Leicester. The site was the former location of a church. Images of the skeleton were photographed, and a replica was 3D printed. William Shakespeare called the king a hunchback in his play *Richard III*. After the printed skeleton was studied, it was determined that the king suffered from scoliosis, which is curvature of

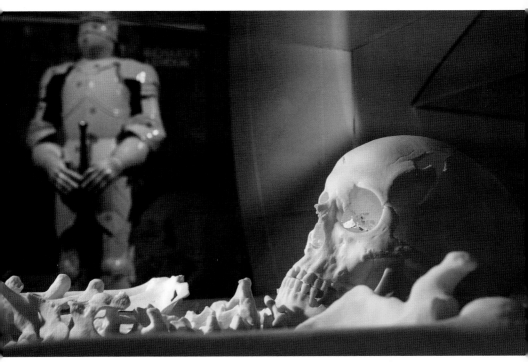

A 3D-printed reconstruction of the skeleton of King Richard III helps people understand how the man lived and died.

the spine. There were also marks seen on the bones that showed wounds that were the cause of death. The skull was used to make a facial reconstruction of the man who died more than five hundred years ago so we can see what he looked like.

Fingerprint Examination

Powder and tape together have proved useful in collecting fingerprints from crime scenes, but these flat materials capturing flat prints do not take into account the curves of fingers. A 3D model can more exactly show the mark a finger makes. An investigator is no longer looking at a fingerprint but at a model of a finger. This can also benefit jurors. Investigators can more easily highlight unique indicators on a 3D fingerprint so that jurors can more easily see them. A 3D model of a fingerprint can be printed much larger than the original fingerprint, but the detail doesn't get distorted with the increase in size. This can also benefit forensics students. By feeling the patterns of ridges and valleys in a print, they can better "see" how prints differ from each other and understand what markers to look for when examining a print. They'll be better prepared when they're working a job that calls on them to read a print.

Forensic Pathology

Virtopsy, introduced at the University of Bern, Switzerland, allows investigators to study bullets or particle fragments lodged in a living body without putting that life in danger, or lodged in clothing without disturbing the delicate cloth environment. They can take a CT scan of the body or clothing and then use the data from that to create a 3D-printed model of the bullet. This also helps jurors, who can see a physical representation of the bullet, not just a CT image of it.

Bones

A 2015 *Forbes* article talked about one of the last places the field is opening to the advantages of 3D printing: digitizing and printing human bones. As three-dimensional objects, bones, like fingerprints, can't be photographed to the quality that those working in police and criminal justice jobs find ideal. That's why forensics experts are increasingly becoming interested in 3D printing bones. Though there aren't many legal restrictions on digitizing human bones in the United States, there are ethical questions about doing so, and that means the exploration of the application of this technology has to progress alongside discussions of ethics.

It doesn't matter that the bones belong to people who are dead. They're still part of humans and, therefore, subject to concerns such as those of social justice. "Justice in access is a reasonable question to raise in light of 3D printing's use in forensic cases," **bioarchaeologist** Kristina Killgrove wrote in *Forbes*. "Which cases will be able to afford such technology? Will the technology be applied correctly and fairly? Will it bias the jury or help?"

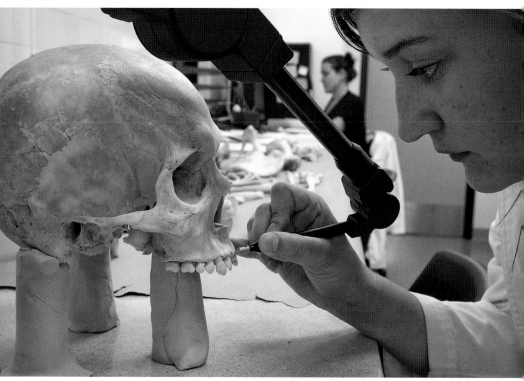

A graduate student hopes to identify bones using 3D-printed models.

Digitised Diseases, an online database of digitized human bones, does not allow its images to be 3D printed. The bones, all of which have been affected by chronic disease, are from archaeological and historical medical collections. They were collected under a license from the United Kingdom's Human Tissue Authority, so printing the models for any purpose, even education, in considered misuse. In the United States, the Native American Graves Protection and Repatriation Act, which provides rules on how researchers and the public must handle Native American sites, artifacts, and human remains, does not say specifically that digitization of artifacts and bones can't happen.

Writing in *Forbes*, Killgrove said there's clearly a need for all organizations to "move towards clarifying the collective stance on this research in coming years." In pressing, time-sensitive matters, murder trials could benefit from the presentation of bones as evidence. Photographs don't do three-dimensional bones justice in such cases. Killgrove quoted biological anthropologist David Errickson as saying that presenting actual bones to juries can be "disturbing" to the point of "prejudicing the jury." He also cautioned that passing delicate evidence such as bones around in a courtroom could damage the evidence. This is where 3D printing can really help.

Killgrove wrote of a May 2015 murder conviction in the United Kingdom that she believed happened in part because of the use of 3D-printed bones. Investigators and prosecutors digitally scanned a fragment of bone found at the defendant's house as well as one found at a crime scene. By digitally moving the fragments, investigators could see how they originally had belonged to the same bone. A 3D scan matched a specific weapon to cuts on the bone. During the trial, the jury got to see all of this through projected 3D images and through examining the 3D printed bones.

Killgrove also described 3D printing's usefulness in the field of biological anthropology. Bioarchaeologists work with human bones hundreds or thousands of years

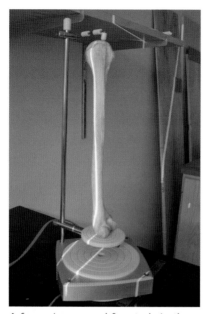
A femur is scanned for study in the lab of Kristina Killgrove.

old, but what they learn from how those people died helps them understand how people are living and dying still today. Killgrove explained: "Reconstructing the trajectory of blunt force trauma to a Middle Pleistocene hominin skull gives us new information into the history of human interpersonal violence; digitizing ancient European bone affected by leprosy provides a window into disability and caregiving in the past; and printing out bones that are often missing in medical-grade teaching skeletons, such as the hyoid or the coccyx, furthers the education of students of osteology and medicine."

Even mummies are being studied with 3D printing. In 2015, a child who had been naturally mummified 550 years ago, meaning that the conditions in which she was buried preserved her, even the skin of her ears, was found in Peru. The remains were brought to the radiology department at Cincinnati Children's Hospital Medical Center in Ohio. Killgrove said there's a lack of children's skeletons in teaching collections, so this discovery was exciting for that reason. The radiologists took X-rays (producing two-dimensional images) and CT scans (producing three-dimensional ones) of the mummy and discovered she was a little girl about two or three years old at the time of her death. By examining the twelve thousand images they produced, they noticed a hole in her spine, which they thought may have contributed to her death. To be certain, they 3D printed models of that area. According to 3DPrint.com, because of those printed objects, the doctors changed their hypothesis and determined that the hole was made after the girl was already dead.

Careers in 3D Printing

According to a 2013 article in *Business News Daily*, the 3D printing job sector is growing like nothing we've seen before. A 2012 MyCorporation infographic estimated that it would become a $5.2 billion industry by 2020, with a projected 14 percent annual growth between 2012 and 2017, making its growth "unprecedented," according to Freelancer.com. In his 2013 State of the Union address, President Barack Obama singled out 3D printing for its "potential to revolutionize the way we make almost everything."

Not only does this mean more workers will be needed to meet demand, but new types of jobs will be created. For example, people may have already worked for decades in computer-aided design (CAD), but whole new roles, like biomedical modeling, can be found in designing for 3D. Also, old jobs will find new audiences. Lawyers and accountants, for example, are needed in the field of 3D printing. People's skills and talents will not be isolated to one area of 3D printing but will be required in all types of 3D printing companies, including vendors, manufacturers, and retail stores.

Following are some jobs that *Business News Daily* says will "be created or get a boost" because of 3D printing's popularity.

1. 3D Design

You can't print without a drawing, template, or model. The computer must be able to read instructions, like a 3D image, in order to know what you want. This means every 3D project must involve a 3D designer.

These people must be imaginative and possess drawing and mathematical skills. They must have the ability to calculate angles, see the simple shapes behind complex-looking objects, and understand if an idea can successfully translate from screen to real life. Designers must also be able to communicate and work with others because they often create 3D designs at the request of clients. They have to know the right questions to ask a client to draw out what that client wants and be able to explain what it will take to make that idea reality. For example, Shapeways is a 3D printing business. It prints on demand for its customers just as a business card printer will print whatever text and logo a business submits. Yet Shapeways still employs people who check those designs to make sure they can exist as objects. These people receive the submitted design and then check its dimensions, asking if the item will be able to exist, physically, based on this design. If there are any moving parts, they confirm that they're designed so that they won't knock into each other or anything else.

3D printers are being used in many design-based disciplines: product design, medical device design, architectural visualization, and entertainment design, Erol Gunduz told *Business News Daily*. He's a professor at New York University's School of Professional Studies, which offers programs in 3D printing, design, and modeling. Any high school or college student focusing on design of any kind would benefit from gaining hands-on experience in 3D technology and staying up-to-date on how companies use 3D printing. "This gives them a significant advantage when looking for career opportunities within creative fields," Gunduz told the newspaper. Not only does this open more doors to careers, but it enhances a person's practice, even if his or her work doesn't require 3D imaging or printing.

Danit Peleg, Jessica Rosenkrantz, and Jesse Louis-Rosenberg, all designers of 3D-printed clothing, attended school beyond high school. Peleg graduated from the Shenkar College of Design, focusing on art but open to technology. She made 3D-printed garments part of her schoolwork. Rosenkrantz and Louis-Rosenberg–mentioned in chapter 3–founded Nervous System, which deliberately meshes art and technology, designing 3D-printed objects and working with the public to design their own ideas. The founders' educational backgrounds set them up well for this work: Rosenkrantz graduated from MIT with degrees in architecture and biology and then studied architecture at the Harvard Graduate School of Design. Louis-Rosenberg majored in mathematics at MIT and then, before founding Nervous System, honed his art-plus-technology sensibilities as a consultant in building modeling and design automation for Gehry Technologies.

Design student Danit Peleg speaks to fashion bloggers about her 3D-printed fashion collection.

Matt Donley, who runs MasterSketchup.com, a website of tutorials for designing with SketchUp, has a background in construction. This made him "naturally inspired," he said, to see the 3D images behind the 3D reality he was building. One day in 2007, he was playing a video game when he saw buried within the game system folders a file named Build.exe. He clicked on it and found a map editor that allowed him to modify the game, adding his own levels. Without formal education in design software, he started experimenting with SketchUp, practicing by drawing remodeling jobs he was working on. He found that his SketchUp designs were a great way to communicate issues to his design team.

2. 3D Computer-Aided Design Modeling

Though designers need to be familiar with software and other technologies, specialists like CAD experts help the design process move smoothly. They convert product designs into the blueprints that 3D printers need in order to build. Their role is particularly important when a company is making individualized projects because they become experts in their field's most common feature sizes, geometrical constraints, and materials. Bespoke Innovations, which 3D designs and prints prosthetic leg covers, is one such company. Alex English is the owner of ProtoParadigm, a 3D printing business that also performs research and development on 3D printing hardware and new printing materials. He told *Business News Daily*, "Bespoke manufacturing and custom prototyping both rely on the user's ability to conceptualize the object they want and accurately create its digital representation ... I see a lot more demand for CAD and 3D modeling jobs on the horizon because of 3D printing."

3. Research and Development

Nothing mentioned in this book–none of the products, inventions, or technological advancements–would have existed without people working in research and development (R&D). *Business News Daily* explained, "Jobs will also open up for forward-thinking R&D professionals who understand the intersection of tech and consumer products while keeping an eye on the bottom line." A technology like 3D printing can make innovative products only to the extent that humans can dream them. Humans also must be able to experiment, testing and refining those dreams into a process a 3D printer can feasibly follow. They must fit a budget as well.

"The ability to visualize a line of fashion accessories or jewelry designs before committing to working with expensive materials affords an advantage for companies to reduce costs in development cycles," Gunduz told *Business News Daily.*

4. Biological and Scientific Modeling

As has been discussed, engineers, designers, and modelers can find new jobs in the field of 3D printing and also would benefit from understanding the technology no matter their current job. They can focus their discipline in other ways as well, such as studying biomedicine. The technology of 3D printing is becoming ever more important in making prostheses, repairing nerves, and crafting medical supplies such as medicine and devices with which to administer that medicine, and those fields will be the particularly well paying, or "high end," as Alex English said.

5. Education

Kids as young as kindergarten are being exposed in school, at least, to 3D printing. Fab labs are finding funding in high schools, allowing students to fabricate, or make, items using 3D printing technology. Colleges and universities are launching 3D printing courses and certificate programs. New York University offers a certificate in 3D printing rapid prototyping. This means teachers who understand the technology and can convey that knowledge in specialized courses are in great demand. They must also be willing and able to continuously educate themselves. Technology moves fast, and in order to provide a good education in 3D printing, teachers must be able to address the latest advancements and obstacles. Danit Peleg even gave a TED talk on the subject, educating the mainstream. The 3D engineers, designers, and CAD experts of tomorrow must be taught those skills today—as must the future consumers and benefactors of 3D-printed products.

6. Lawyers and Legal Professionals

Products made from 3D designs are subject to intellectual property (IP) laws, and because 3D printing aims to be an accessible technology, widely used across fields, there's a lot of work for lawyers and other legal professionals to do.

"As 3D printing technologies advance and become more widely accessible, it will be easier for infringers to create, market, and sell products that infringe patents, copyrights, and valuable brands," Julie Matthews, partner at the law firm Edwards Wildman, told *Business News Daily*. Whole new business models, built on copying and modifying products, will spring up, she said.

Lawyers will bring forth and defend against IP enforcement actions and lawsuits regarding IP ownership, scope of rights, licensing, fair use, and international rights, among other forms of IP protection. Legal professionals will also stay busy monitoring infringements. However, with the open-source community sharing information willingly with everyone, IP laws could be rendered obsolete.

7. Business Opportunities

People with business degrees and those with the entrepreneurial spirit can start or franchise their own 3D printing business. With top-of-the-line commercial 3D printers costing as little as $2,000, and print shops being able to exist online only, overhead can be nominal, or small. In 2013, UPS launched a pilot program at two of its retail stores, testing 3D printing as a service offered alongside document printing, copying, and shipping. Soon, 3D printing will be "just another" option offered locally, alongside ice cream shops, cell phone stores, and car dealerships.

These new companies or storefronts will need support staff, not just business owners or technical staff. More jobs in operations, administration, data analysis, and sales will be created if 3D printing grows as an everyday service. Manual laborers will also be needed. Shapeways, a major 3D printing company, employs people who work in the packing and shipping department. The printed objects have to somehow be delivered to the people who designed and paid for them to be built! Shapeways also has staff to carefully finish the printed product, removing it from the supporting material, cleaning it, and providing quality control.

"The businesses that will spring up with new business models centered on 3D printing will also have a need for more common jobs that other businesses need, like marketing, clerical, shipping, et cetera," English told *Business News Daily*.

GLOSSARY

additive manufacturing Creating objects by adding material layer by layer; another name for 3D printing.

additive process The way in which an object is built layer by layer. There are many 3D printing processes.

bioarchaeologist Someone who studies human remains from archaeological sites.

bioprinting 3D printing with living cells to create living tissue, organs, and other body parts.

build bed The flat part of the 3D printer on which an object is printed. Also called a printer bed.

casting Making an object by pouring material, like molten metal, into a mold often made of sand.

computer-aided design (CAD) Architects, engineers, and others use CAD software to draw objects in three dimensions they want to 3D print.

extrude To push or force out a material, like filament, through a nozzle to form a continuous ribbon.

filament Material used to 3D print an object, usually a plastic wound on a spool.

4D printing Making objects that change their shape when removed from the 3D printer. Having four dimensions means to have length/width, depth, height, and transformation.

fused deposition modeling (FDM) A trademarked term that refers to one of the most widely used methods of 3D printing. FDM 3D printers heat a thermoplastic filament to its melting point and then extrude it, layer by layer, to create an object.

G-code A computer programming language mainly used in computer-aided manufacturing. The code sends directions to a printer to provide a path for the extruding nozzle.

laser sintering (LS) A type of 3D printing. In this technology, a precisely guided laser beam binds layers of solid powder materials, typically plastics. Sintering is joining things by heat without melting.

layer The material put down in a certain thickness by a 3D printer on one pass over an object it is printing to build up the object a little at a time.

nozzle Part of the printing head through which material is extruded.

open-source projects Objects that can be built using original source code for software that is freely available for use, redistribution, and modification.

polyethylene A thermoplastic polymer used for everything from grocery bags to drain pipes.

prosthesis An artificial body part such as a hand.

prototype A first or typical model of something from which other items are developed or copied.

scaffolding A structure printed to support transplanted cells until they eventually can support themselves.

skull photographic superimposition A forensics technique used in conjunction with 3D printing; researchers compare recovered human remains with photographs of people who have gone missing to determine identity.

slicer This software "slices" a 3D image into layers, which can then be coded for printing the 3D image into an object, one layer at a time.

software Programs that operate 3D printers and other computer-guided objects; contrast with "hardware," which is the 3D printer itself.

sparse fill A 3D printing technique that allows the printed object to appear solid from the outside but the inside is a grid like a honeycomb.

STL 3D modeling software files are saved in the STL (stereolithography) file format, which can then be converted to G-code, which 3D printers use to print objects.

subtractive manufacturing Creating an object by removing material from around it.

thermoplastics A family of plastics that can be heated into liquid and cooled into solid. Frozen, thermoplastics become like glass. Thermoplastics can be reheated, reshaped, and frozen repeatedly.

3D Having three dimensions: length/width, depth, and height.

3D sand printing A technique that uses resin to glue together layers of sand in order to print detailed molds in which to make metal objects.

triangular mesh Used in computer graphics, this is a set of triangles connected by their common edges or corners to make 3D objects.

Virtopsy A trademarked term for a virtual autopsy that uses CT scans and 3D-printed objects; it can also be used to investigate injuries on living humans.

watertight An object is watertight when the 3D printer can tell the inside from the outside of the model.

FURTHER INFORMATION

Companies and Organizations

e-Nable

http://enablingthefuture.org/about

The e-Nable community spans the globe. It gets together to find ways to improve the open-source designs for 3D printable hand and arm prostheses. Visit to find out ways to get involved.

GrabCAD

https://grabcad.com

Since 2010, GrabCAD has offered product designers, engineers, manufacturing professionals, and anyone interested in 3D printing, including students, an online community. People share CAD files and models, discuss challenges, and share tips. CAD stands for "computer-aided design," and CAD software is useful when designing for 3D printers.

MeshLab

http://www.meshlab.net

This is an open-source system for processing and editing 3D triangular meshes.

Nervous System

http://n-e-r-v-o-u-s.com

This design studio, founded in 2007, combines technology and art, along with inspiration from the natural world, to create products. It also encourages customers to participate in the design process by using its apps.

Pinshape

https://pinshape.com

This 3D printing community and marketplace offers lots of information and products for free and for sale.

Plastic Scribbler

http://www.plasticscribbler.com

This company offers customers tutorials, troubleshooting guides, forums, affordable 3D printers, and other products to make home 3D printing as easy as possible.

Shapeways

https://www.shapeways.com

Anyone can upload a design with Shapeways, and the company will 3D print it and can help with marketing and selling it.

SketchUp

https://www.sketchup.com

SketchUp provides free 3D modeling software designed for people to use even at home.

Thingiverse

http://www.thingiverse.com

MakerBot's Thingiverse is a design community for people making 3D-printed objects. They encourage all designs uploaded to be licensed under a Creative Commons license, meaning the design is open source and anyone can use or alter any design.

Videos

Direct Metal Laser Printing–Jay Leno's Garage.

https://www.youtube.com/watch?v=bwFspzVGUF4

Watch a February 2017 segment of *Jay Leno's Garage* on 3D printing car parts.

Forget Shopping.
Soon You'll Download Your New Clothes

https://www.ted.com/talks/danit_peleg_
forget_shopping_soon_you_ll_download_
your_new_clothes/transcript?language=en

In this TEDYouth talk, fashion designer Danit Peleg tells how her senior project turned into a new-age fashion line.

Here's a Simple Video Tutorial to 3D Print a World of Warcraft Model—Like Swift Spectral Tiger

https://3dprint.com/121451/3d-printed-world-of-warcraft

This step-by-step written and video tutorial from 3dprint.com shows how to 3D print a World of Warcraft character.

How 3D Printing Works

https://www.youtube.com/watch?v=BTTnaI4EYnY&feature=youtu.be

This short video was made for potential Shapeways customers but also serves as a good overview of the entire 3D printing process, including what the printers look like, what materials are used, and what people work in 3D manufacturing.

Kinematics Dress by Nervous System—3D Printed

https://www.youtube.com/watch?v=wdRswasftfI

Shapeways shows the 3D printing of a wearable dress.

The Science Behind the Mummy

https://www.youtube.com/watch?v=h17NB8X4-0w&feature=youtube

Learn about a multidisciplinary study of a baby mummy through the use of 3D printing technology.

Sketchup Tutorial: How to Create a Vase

https://mastersketchup.com/sketchup-tutorial-how-to-create-a-vase

Matt Donley, founder of MasterSketchup.com, offers a written and video tutorial on designing a vase for 3D printing.

3D-Printed "Magic Arms"

https://www.youtube.com/watch?v=WoZ2BgPVtA0

In this short video from Stratasys, watch Emma Lavelle use her magic arms.

3D-Printed Ovaries Produce Healthy Offspring

https://www.youtube.com/watch?v=_5whpjlPO6Q

Northwestern University explains how researchers are using 3D printing to create the "ovary of the future."

3D Printer Builds Homes from Mud in Impoverished Areas

http://www.iflscience.com/technology/3d-printer-uses-mud-natural-fibers-make-homes-impoverished-areas

This video shows a mud house–building 3D printer in action.

Websites

Digitised Diseases

http://www.digitiseddiseases.org/alpha

This online resource from the University of Bradford in the United Kingdom allows anyone to search 3D images of human bones that have been affected by diseases.

Inverse.com

https://www.inverse.com/article/5885-mit-figured-out-how-to-3d-print-glass-and-it-s-stunning

In one video embedded in this story titled "MIT Figured Out How to 3D Print Glass and It's Stunning," you can watch glass being printed, and in the other, you can learn more about the MIT Glass Lab, which is partly responsible for this advancement in 3D printing.

Nghia Vuong's Ring

https://grabcad.com/library/engagement-ring-project-1

Nghia Vuong, who 3D printed an engagement ring for his girlfriend, shared CAD models for a baseline prototype ring.

Virtual Curation Laboratory

https://vcuarchaeology3d.wordpress.com/about

The Virtual Curation Laboratory is a catalog of artifacts from sites such as Jamestown, George Washington's Ferry Farm, and James Madison's Montpelier.

INDEX

Page numbers in **boldface** are illustrations. Entries in **boldface** are glossary terms.

accident reconstruction, 96–98

additive process, 5

aerogel, 47

aphantasia, 17–18

architecture, 13, **24**, 25–34, 44–47

art, 21–22, 30, **30**, 46, 50–51, **51**, 53, 107–108

athletics, 65, **86**, 87

automotive industry, 13, 25, 34–36,

aviation industry, 8, **8**, 36–40

Bespoke Innovations, 87–88, 109–110

binder jetting, 95

bioarchaeologist, 101, 103–105

bioprinting, **70**, 72, 76–85, **80**, **82**

Boeing, 8, **8**, 36, 38–39

bones, 33, 97–105, **99**, **102**

Borcher, Kirsten, 79

build bed, 5, 9–11

Burrus, Daniel, 49, 63–65

Campos, Eric Octavio, 20–21

carbon emissions, 37

careers, 105–113

casting, 34, 38, 62, 68, 98

ceramics, 57, 84

clothing, 58–61, **59**, 63, 107–108, **108**

computer-aided design (CAD), 10, 15, 28, 34, 43, 52, 105, 109–111

Crump, Lisa, 12–13

Crump, S. Scott, 12–13

death masks, 50

Dini, Enrico, 31–33

directed energy deposition, 95

disruptive technology, 6

Donley, Matt, 57–58, 109

D-Shape, 31–33

education, 13, 17–19, 111

Enable UC, 72–74, **73**

Evenhuis, Jiri, 61

exoskeleton, 85–87

extrude, 5, 11, 14, 23, 30, 46, 51, 60, 64, 79, 95

fairings, 87–88

Felix, Allyson, 65

filament, 10, 15, 41, 78

film industry, 47, **48**, 66–68, **68**

fingerprints, 100–101

fisheye lens, 19

food, 60

Ford, 35–36

forensics, 95–101, **97**

4D printing, 53, 58

fused deposition modeling (FDM), 36, 41, 52, 69

G-code, 10–11, 17, 43, 54

gelatin, 79–80, **80**

General Electric, 8, 38–39

glass, 14, 50–51, 53–54

guns, 93–94

Hadid, Zaha, 29–30

Hakes, Julian, 66

hawk moths, 21

Hypernom, 19

ice, **24**, 44–47

Industrial Revolution, 29

intellectual property law, 112

International Space Station (ISS), 40–41, 43

jaw, 84–85, 96

jewelry, 62–63, **62**, 110

juries, 95, 100–101, 103

Killgrove, Kristina, 101, 103–105

Kinematics, 58–60

Kyttanen, Janne, 61

Laronda, Monica, 81

laser sintering (LS), 33–35

LayerWise, 84

Leno, Jay, 34, **35**

lenses, 19, 53

leveling, 10

Louis-Rosenberg, Jesse, 58–61, 107–108

Luis, Lira, 26

Made in China 2025,
39–40
Made in Space, 40–41, **42**,
43
"magic arms," 85–87
Mann, Geoffrey, 21–22
manufacturing, 14–16
Mars Ice House, **24**, 44–47
Masanet, Eric, 37
mathematics, 16–19, 59, 71,
88, 106
medical supplies, 88–90
medication, 90–91
Meijs, Piet, 26–29
metal, 14, 16, 34–35, 37–
38, 40, 62, 84, 93–95
microprocessors, 53
Miyake, Issey, 61, 63
mummies, 104–105
museums, 50, **51**, 58, 61,
68–69

NASA, 40–41, 43–44
nerves, 74, 82–84, **82**, 111
Nervous System, 58–61,
107–108
nozzle, 5, 10, 32, 39, 47, 51

open-source projects, 9,
54–55, 73, 89, 93, 112

organs, 77–81, **92**
ovaries, 76–81, **80**
Oxman, Neri, 22–23, 29,
33–34, 50, 54

Peleg, Danit, 107, **108**, 111
plastic, 5, 7, 9–12, 14, 16,
22, 30, 33, 52, 56–58,
60, 62, 69, 74, 78–79,
86, 94
pollinators, 20–21
polyethylene, 12
powder bed fusion, 95
prosthesis, 72–76, **73**, **76**,
84, **86**, 87–88, 109, 111
prototype, 12, 14–16, 26,
36, 38, 64, 66, 109–111

reactionware, 90
Reichental, Abraham, 6, 8
Reinersten, Sarah, **86**,
87–88
research and
development, 109–110
Richard III, 99–100, **99**
Rosenkrantz, Jessica,
58–61, 107–108
Royal BAM Group, 33
Rutz, Alexandra, 77–78

scaffolding, **80**, 81

scanning, 69, 83, 86–87, 96, 101, 103, **104**, 105

Segerman, Henry, 17–19, **18**

Shah, Ramille, 80

Shapeways, 59–61, 106–107, 113

shoes, 63–66

silkworms, 22–23

SketchUp, 26, 56–57, 109

skull photographic superimposition, 98–99

slicer, 9–11

Smithsonian Institution, 68–69

Softkill Design, 33

software, 9–11, 14, 16, 26, 34, 61, 65, 91, 109

space exploration, **24**, 25, 39–41, 43–47

sparse fill, 52, 57, 69

spools, 11, 15

stereographic projection, 18–19, **18**

STL, 11, 55

Stratasys, 12–13, 15, 26, 34, 50, 52

subtractive manufacturing, 9

syringe pumps, 89–90, 93

thermoplastics, 16, 52, 69

3D sand printing, 36

3D Systems, 6, 61

throwaway culture, 6–7

titanium, 34, 37–38, 84

triangular mesh, 55

Universe Architecture, 30–31, 33

Virtopsy, 100–101

watertight, 11, 56

Williams, Amy, 65–66, **66**

Woodruff, Teresa, 77, 80

World of Warcraft, 54–55

ABOUT THE AUTHOR

KRISTIN THIEL is a writer and editor based in Portland, Oregon. Her first book with Cavendish Square was on Dorothy Hodgkin, a Nobel Prize–winning chemist and pioneer in X-ray crystallography. She has worked on many of the books in the So, You Want to Be A … series (Aladdin/Beyond Words), which offers career guidance for kids. She was the lead writer on a report for her city about funding for high school dropout prevention. Thiel has judged YA book contests and helped start a Kids Voting USA affiliate. She has been a substitute teacher in grades K–12 and managed before-school and after-school literacy programs for AmeriCorps VISTA.